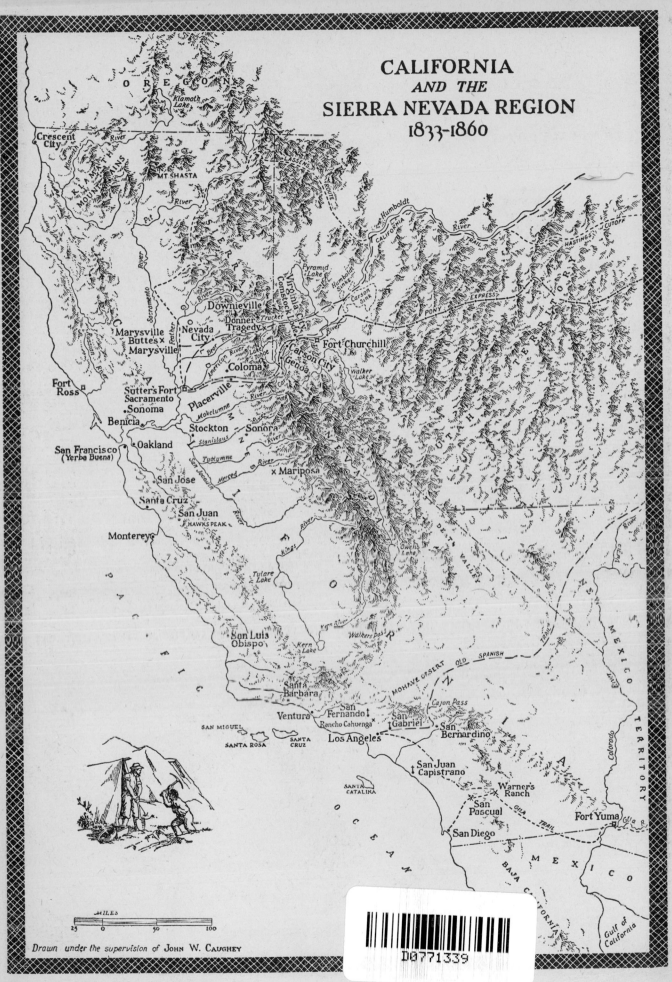

# CALIFORNIA
## *AND THE*
# SIERRA NEVADA REGION
### 1833-1860

*Drawn under the supervision of* JOHN W. CAUGHEY

D0771339

# ALBUM

_Joseph Henry Jackson_

# GOLD RUSH ALBUM

## JOSEPH HENRY JACKSON

**Editor in Chief**

CHARLES SCRIBNER'S SONS • NEW YORK
1949

# FOREWORD

A T the beginning of the year 1849 one topic was uppermost in men's minds everywhere—the gold fields of California.

There was reason enough for this. America was fidgety, for one thing. Young men, only a generation away from the excitements of their country's pioneering beginnings, were growing weary of the counting-house, the rocky New England farms, the dawn-to-dark hard labor of making a living on the new lands their fathers had broken to the plow on what was then thought to be the extreme frontier. The Mexican War was over, too, and had left a new spirit of restlessness in its wake. Now, providentially, here was a fresh adventure. In California a man might pick up his everlasting fortune for no more than the trouble of the bending over. Gold, as it has always been, was a powerful word, a charm to unlock who knew how many gates.

As the year began, the New York *Herald* described the state of affairs accurately in the circumlocutory journalese of the day:

"The excitement relative to the gold fields of California," wrote its editor, "continues with unabated fervor. It is daily fed with all sorts of reports. Every statement is caught up and swallowed with the greatest avidity . . . all are rushing head over heels towards the El Dorado on the Pacific—that wonderful California, which sets the public mind almost on the highway to insanity. Every day men of property and means are advertising their possessions for sale, in order to furnish them with means to reach that golden land. Every little city and town beyond the great seaports, or within their reach, is forming societies either to cross the isthmus or to double Cape Horn."

The *Herald's* editor added the perhaps superfluous note that husbands were preparing to leave their wives, that sons were saying farewell to their mothers, and—it was evidently worth commenting upon—that "bachelors are parting with their comforts," to go to the gold fields. He did not exaggerate. That rush of 1849 was America's first great migration.

There had been a beginning in 1848, to be sure. Gold was discovered at the very beginning of that year, and the news soon leaked out in spite of the efforts of interested people to keep it quiet. By the latter part of May, Sutter, on whose land the discovery had been made, was writing in his diary, "Hosts arriving by water and land for the Mts." Down in the sleepy capital at Monterey, Walter Colton complained that "The blacksmith dropped his hammer, the carpenter his plane, the mason his trowel, the baker his loaf." People, he said, were going even on crutches, and he records that one was carried on a litter. At the *presidio* of Monterey soldiers slipped away. Sailors left their ships by the hundreds. By the first of June there were two thousand miners digging and washing in the hills. In another month there were four thousand. Most of these were Californians; the news had not taken hold yet in the east.

Then, in November, the east woke up. Horace Greeley had his say: "We are on the brink of an Age of Gold!" he declared, and went on to estimate that within the next four years California would add "at least one thousand millions of dollars to the general aggregate of gold in circulation in the world." Mr. Greeley missed it by a good deal; the total for the period he named, which includes the bonanza year of 1852, ran something over two hundred millions of dollars. But even the hint of such sums was enough to set Americans moving.

Just how many came to California in those first few years is a matter of estimate. The best figures show that at the end of 1848 California held some 20,000 persons, not counting Indians. At the end of 1849 the population was close to 100,000. By the latter part of 1852 it was about 225,000. Many of these were Latin Americans, French, Germans, Englishmen, Australians and even Chinese. But the shift in population within the borders of the United States itself was sufficient to be of extraordinary importance.

In this book the reader has a chance to go along with the American-in-search-of-his-fortune, to accompany him (and often his family and farm animals), by the various routes he took to California. By the Overland Trail, so called, by the Santa Fe Trail, (and the variants of both), via the Isthmus of Panama and around the Horn, the American came to take possession of his country's newest outpost. Here the reader will discover what that journey was like, whatever route the Argonaut chose.

It is true, of course, that those who came to California's gold fields did not expect to remain; at least most of them certainly did not. Over and again the record shows the fact; diaries, letters, journals all make a point of returning to "the States" once the pile was made. California was simply the easy road to wealth.

Very few of the Argonauts found it that. And this book will provide a glimpse of some of the reasons why. Mining turned out not to be quite the simple affair the high-hearted, cocksure boys and young men thought. You might not find a gold deposit at all. If you did, and staked it out, you had to have water, and in the summer water took some getting. Or you discovered that in the deep river canyons, where there was also gold, you had to stand waist-deep in the icy stream for days on end and then perhaps found no more gold than you might have earned at the plow back home. Maybe you did well; you found both gold and water together, and you came to the end of the day with ten or perhaps fifty times the sum you could have made in the east for the same number of hours of labor. Then you realized that you had to spend it all, just in order to keep alive. Every necessity had to be packed up into the hills from the cities down below, and with eggs a dollar each and flour at a hundred dollars a barrel your takings went faster than you could accumulate them. No, the fortunes were not so easy to pick up as the stories had made it seem.

So it happened that the men of the gold rush stayed, or at least many thousands of them did. And they were the men who, when the hysterical rush was over and gold mining had become a business like any other, found opportunities in California's valleys rather than its hills, and built up the agricultural and industrial empire that their State so quickly became. This book, since its purpose is to delineate the rush itself, does no more than suggest that significant metamorphosis of California. It does not need to do more, really, for some millions of Americans, in a later and greater series of migrations westward, have made that discovery for themselves.

In 1948, 1949, and 1950, the State of California celebrates its three centennial anniversaries of the Discovery, the Rush, and Statehood. This *Gold Rush Album,* therefore, comes at precisely the right time. For California's celebrations are peculiarly the nation's as well. Only a century ago there were hardly any Californians at all; the State's ten million people came to California, most of them, from the rest of the country—came and stayed to make a great State out of what they realized, for one reason or another, was a Golden Land. Here, in a form as vivid as we could make it, is the text-and-picture story of how the earliest of those millions got here. It is a narrative of importance to all Americans.

Berkeley, California
January 1, 1949

JOSEPH HENRY JACKSON

# ACKNOWLEDGMENT

In securing these pictures, most of which are contemporary and many by actual participants, generous and expert assistance of libraries, museums and historical societies in the persons of their Directors and the members of their staffs has been indispensable. Specific credit accompanies each picture, but particular mention is due to the following:

The Bancroft Library, University of California, and Mr. George P. Hammond, Director.

The California Historical Society, San Francisco, California, and Mrs. Edna Martin Parratt, Managing Director.

The California State Library, Sacramento, California; Miss Mabel R. Gillis, State Librarian, and Miss Caroline Wenzel.

The Henry E. Huntington Library and Art Gallery, San Marino, California, and Dr. Leslie E. Bliss, Librarian.

The New-York Historical Society, New York City; Mr. R. W. G. Vail, the Director; Miss Dorothy Barck, Mr. Arthur Carlson and Miss Betty Ezequelle.

The New York Public Library, New York City; the Messrs. Sylvester Vigilante and F. Ivor D. Avellino, and the staff of the Photographic Department.

The Society of California Pioneers, San Francisco, California; the Misses Hazel M. Ball and Helen S. Giffen.

The Wisconsin State Historical Society, Madison, Wisconsin, and Mr. Clifford L. Lord, Director.

We must gratefully acknowledge the advice and assistance of the Misses Georgia W. Read and Ruth Gaines. Messrs. Edward Eberstadt and Sons gave us the benefit of their years of experience in handling Western books and manuscripts, and in addition put the wealth of their stock at our disposal.

# CONTENTS

# GOLD RUSH
# ALBUM

# The Sleepy Utopia

From a painting by Charles Nahl. *Courtesy*, E. B. Crocker Art Gallery, Sacramento, Calif.

EVERY MORNING in California, the dew settled on the petals of acres of roses, to become hard and candied like a sweet and heavenly manna.

The few, enervated Spaniards who dwelt there gave themselves over to the joys of the *fandango*, and left the care of their vast cattle herds to faithful *vaqueros*. These were a people made to be ruled.

Any upstanding American who came to California could take what land he pleased in this terrestrial paradise. No one was ever sick in California and few died. Corn yielded seventy to eighty-fold in this gracious earth. Exotic fish teemed in the rivers, bays and lakes.

Best of all, as the year 1848 dawned, the flag of the United States waved and would wave for all time over the evergreen valleys drowsing in perpetual summer beneath snow-capped guardian peaks.

So they told us, and we believed them.

Alexander Forbes, *California: A History of Upper and Lower California.* 1839

Other nations had coveted Mexico's one-time province. As early as 1839, Forbes, the British consul down the coast at Tepic, had been moving heaven and earth to pack his countrymen into California. The view of the Mission of San Francisco *above* appeared in a book he wrote to encourage English immigration.

Just as General Scott was storming the heights of Chapultepec, an enterprising New York editor passed off the picture *below* as a genuine view of the town of San Francisco, formerly known as "the settlement at Yerba Buena cove."

William Arthur, ed., *The Antiquarian and General Review.* 1847

Weary men and women who had gone to Oregon in the early Forties could have told us the truth about the crossing of a continent. The fur traders and Mountain Men, and the sea captains who traded dry goods, hardware and square pianos at Monterey for hides and tallow could have told us the truth about California. But people like these didn't write books or draw pictures in 1848.

John C. Fremont, *Report of the Exploring Expeditions of 1842 and 1843-44.* 1845

John C. Fremont, *Report of the Exploring Expeditions of 1842 and 1843-44.* 1845

We saw the golden California through the eyes of ambitious men who were dreaming of empire.

Pyramid Lake (*above*) and the snow-filled passes of the Sierra Nevada (*left*) were romantic little drawings which illustrated the triumphant prose of John Charles Fremont's reports to Washington.

"Come, come," cried the adventurers in their guidebooks and published journals! The perils were nothing to Americans, and the rewards would be great. The rich valleys were virgin and unpeopled.

J. R. Bartlett, *Personal Narrative of Explorations.* 1854

J. W. Revere, *A Tour of Duty in California.* 1849

South and west of San Francisco, near Santa Clara (*above*), quicksilver was mined. It was said you might find gold if you took the trouble to look for it.

Meanwhile, there was always sport at the *rodeos* or roundups, where the *vaqueros* showed off their skill with the rope and their horsemanship. The picture *below* shows a *rodeo* near San Francisco at the Mission Dolores.

Friedrich Gerstaecker, *Scenes de la Vie Californienne.* 1859

No one need fear the Indians of California. They were mild and helpless; they lived in huts made of tule rushes and were given to thievery, basket-making, hunting and fishing. To aid them in snaring game they carved and used decoy-birds. (*Right*, the interior of a California Indian hut.)

On certain days they sweat-bathed and climaxed the process by leaping into a cold stream *below*.

J. R. Bartlett, *Personal Narrative of Explorations.* 1854

J. W. Revere, *A Tour of Duty in California.* 1849

Sometimes they fished with spears, but dragnets were used as well.

J. R. Bartlett, *Personal Narrative of Explorations.* 1854

MONTEREY CAPITAL OF CALIFORNIA.

J. W. Revere, *A Tour of Duty in California*. 1849

In 1848, Walter Colton, the *alcalde* or chief magistrate of Monterey (*above*), noted that the town's hospitality was so free a public hotel was hard put to keep open.

The town of San Francisco was prospering in these years. According to some of its inhabitants who were still living in the Eighteen-eighties, the view *below* was a true rendering of how it looked early in 1847 at the time its name was changed from Yerba Buena.

*Courtesy*, Stokes Collection, The New York Public Library

SUTTER'S FORT — NEW HELVETIA.

J. W. Revere, *A Tour of Duty in California.* 1849

Eastward, in the Sacramento Valley, the Swiss adventurer John August Sutter was using the labor of Indians, Kanakas, Mexicans and American wanderers to found a feudal barony on the immense tract of land he had secured from Governor Alvarado. His fort at New Helvetia (*above*) had sheltered Fremont when the Pathfinder had stumbled down the western slope of the Sierra in 1844, more dead than alive.

One of Sutter's many projects was a sawmill to supply lumber for his principality. James W. Marshall set about building one on the south fork of the American River. He and Sutter were to divide the profits of the mill (*below*).

William M'Ilvaine, Jr., *Sketches of Scenery and Notes of Personal Adventure in California & Mexico.* 1850
*Courtesy,* The New-York Historical Society, New York City

VIEW OF CULLOMA.

James Delavan, *Notes on California and the Placers*. 1850. *Courtesy,* The New-York Historical Society, New York City

The work was almost completed at Coloma (*above*) late in January, 1848, but the tail-race was too shallow. Marshall was trying to deepen it by flooding water through it each night. On the morning of January 24, after turning off the water, he stepped down into the ditch to see what progress had been made. There was something shiny on the bedrock under the standing water. It looked like gold. He picked up a nugget.

The camp housekeeper, Mrs. Elizabeth Wimmer, had a kettle of lye boiling for soap-making (*left*). According to her story, she boiled the shiny bit of metal all day and when it did not tarnish, Marshall was sure he had found gold. At Sutter's Fort, Marshall and Sutter made further tests and were convinced. Complete secrecy was sworn, but the word soon got out. Gold— Gold on the American River!

The discoverers had no luck. The erstwhile Baron of the Sacramento spent his old age in futile petitions to Congress for return of his lost acres. Marshall advertised his fame on the printed card shown *below*. He died a poor man; but he and Sutter had started something.

AUTOGRAPH OF

OLD SUTTER MILL

*Jas. W. Marshall*

THE DISCOVERER OF GOLD IN CALIFORNIA

January 19th, 1848

W. W. Allen and R. B. Avery,
*California Gold Book*. 1893

W. W. Allen and R. B. Avery, *California Gold Book*. 1893

Until April, 1848, there was little excitement in the towns along the coast. But as summer drew on, the rush to the American River almost emptied San Jose—San Francisco—even Monterey.

On June 20, *alcalde* Colton observed: "My messenger sent to the mines has returned with specimens of the gold; he dismounted in a sea of upturned faces." In a matter of days, the *alcalde* and the commandant of Monterey were cooking their own food. Every one of those faces was set toward El Dorado.

Walter Colton, *Three Years in California.* 1852

Alonzo Delano, *Old Block's Sketch-Book; or, Tales of California Life.* 1856

On July 18, Colton wrote in explanation of the picture *above*: "A whole platoon of soldiers from the fort deserted and left only the flag behind them." Note the vulture trailing the weary mule.

There was a fine brotherly spirit of co-operation and mutual help among the early miners (*left*).

"Such a mixed and motley crowd—" said Colton of the miners he saw drifting up and down the slopes of the Sierra—"such a restless, roving, rummaging, ragged multitude!"

For the worthy *alcalde* had gone off to the mines himself in September.

Walter Colton, *Three Years in California.* 1852

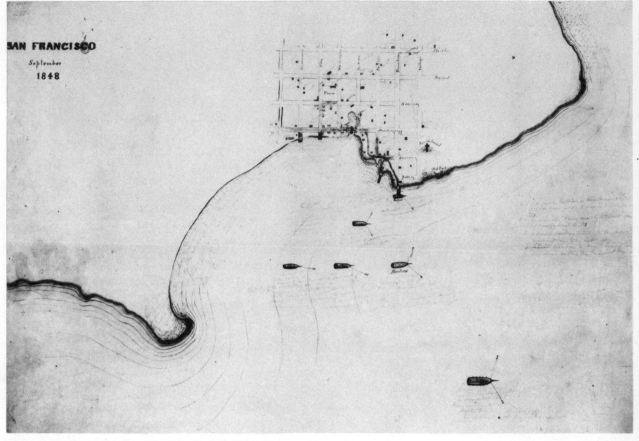

*Courtesy*, Stokes Collection, The New York Public Library

In September, 1848, Augustus Harrison took the brig *Belfast* into the harbor of San Francisco, one of the first traders to come from the Eastern states after the gold rush started. He disposed of his cargo at a roaring profit and took the trouble to draw the plan of the city and harbor shown *above*. The pencil notations were made at a later date. Its neat grid of streets may be compared with the view *below*, drawn in November of the same year by J. C. Ward. All was in readiness now, as the word winged eastward.

Bayard Taylor, *Eldorada, or Adventures in the Path of Empire.* 1850

# 2

# Gold Fever

THE GOLD STRIKE had ceased to be solely a California concern as early as June, 1848, when the news reached Honolulu. By August, settlers barely established in Oregon were making ready to go south for fortune, and the first cautious notices were appearing in newspapers on the eastern coast. People were running about and picking gold out of the California earth the way a thousand loose hogs would root up ground-nuts, said a letter from Monterey to the New York *Journal of Commerce!*

Official news was on the way to Washington. Colonel Richard B. Mason, military governor of California, had sent off on August 17 a careful report of his observations in the mines. The messenger left Monterey and made his way to Peru—thence to Panama and across the Isthmus. From Chagres he sailed for the island of Jamaica, and there got a ship for New Orleans where he let out the golden word and aroused great excitement.

In Washington at last, he delivered the Mason report to the Secretary of War, together with a tea-caddy in which lay lumps and scales of Californian gold to the value of three thousand dollars.

Official Washington saw and believed. The retiring President Polk must have regarded the find as a confirmation of his expansionist policies.

WASHINGTON: WEDNESDAY, DECEMBER 6, 1848.

**PRESIDENT'S ANNUAL MESSAGE.**

A message was received from the President of the United States, by Mr. WALKER, his Private Secretary, which was read by the Secretary, as follows:

It was known that mines of the precious metals existed to a considerable extent in California at the time of its acquisition. Recent discoveries render it probable that these mines are more extensive and valuable than was anticipated. The accounts of the abundance of gold in that Territory are of such an extraordinary character as would scarcely command belief, were they not corroborated by the authentic reports of officers in the public service, who have visited the mineral district, and derived the facts which they detail from personal observation. Reluctant to credit the reports in general circulation as to the quantity of gold, the officer commanding our forces in California visited the mineral district in July last, for the purpose of obtaining accurate information on the subject. His report to the War Department of the result of his examination, and the facts obtained on the spot, is herewith laid before Congress. When he visited the country, there were about four thousand persons engaged in collecting gold. There is every reason to believe that the number of persons so employed has since been augmented. The explorations already made warrant the belief that the supply is very large, and that gold is found at various places in an extensive district of country.

Information received from officers of the navy and other sources, though not so full and minute, confirm the accounts

Mention of Mason's report in Polk's last message of December 5, 1848, and the wide circulation given its content by newspapers sent better than one hundred thousand people in search of El Dorado during 1849 alone.

California would never be again the sleepy land of the ranchers and Indians.

As may be seen *above*, the press of the nation reacted to the news during the two weeks that followed the President's announcement. The great, national restlessness found a focus. *On to California* was the universal cry.

DEFENCE OF THE CALIFORNIA BANK

Broadside cartoons began to appear as the gold fever spread among all classes of society. The artist who made the masterpiece *above* stressed the patriotic character of the rush for California. But a more cynical comment on the excitement is shown *below.*

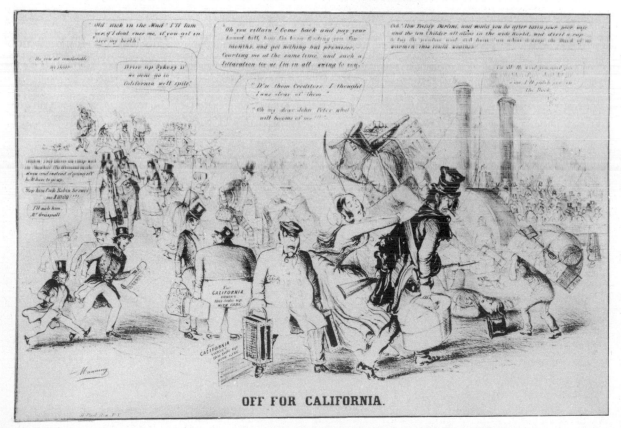

OFF FOR CALIFORNIA.

Both illustrations on this page are by the *courtesy* of The New-York Historical Society, New York City

**GOING TO CALIFORNIA**
via Fremonts route!

Early in 1849, the artist Elton grew prophetic and produced on a single sheet this double cartoon.

RETURNING FROM CALIFORNIA
via Cape Horn!

W. C. Johnson, *Experiences of a Forty Niner.* 1892

The gold rush was more than a flight from responsibility on the part of paunchy failures, would-be great men and recent immigrants. The two young Pennsylvanians *above* were much more typical of the Forty-Niners as a group. Prior to their departure for the great adventure they had themselves daguerreotyped in their trail outfits.

Thousands upon thousands of young men like these read the advertisements at the *right*, considered their qualifications and signed up.

When these "companies" set out on the long journey, they had as a rule a military organization much like that of the State militia.

Very often, the members were presented each with a Bible at the farewell services held by the churches to sanctify the setting forth. The sermon at the *left* was one of hundreds preached as the argonauts departed.

But on the overland trail, or at sea, the secular anthem *below* was the great song of the gold-seekers. Bayard Taylor listened with amazement as his native boatman Juan Crispin roared it out along the Chagres River in the jungles of Panama.

*Courtesy*, The Foster Hall Collection, The University of Pittsburgh, Pa.

### The Best Chance Yet, for
# CALIFORNIA!

A Meeting will be held in COHASSET, at the Office of

## H. J. TURNER,

On SATURDAY, January 27th, at 11 O'Clock, for the purpose of forming a Company, to be called the "South Shore and California Joint Stock Company;" to be composed of 30 Members, and each Member paying $300.

COHASSET, JANUARY 24, 1849.

Propeller Power Presses, 142 Washington St., Boston.

*Courtesy*, Chicago Historical Society, Chicago, Ill.

Rich and aristocratic "companies" went by sea. Many of these groups bought the vessels in which they sailed and owned them in common.

Posters advertised passage to the gold fields on every New England fence and wall.

Note how the same cut of a gallant ship served in both posters on this page; and how life insurance could be "effected on the most advantageous terms and with surety."

The southern states were represented in the rush by sea, as the notice *below* indicates.

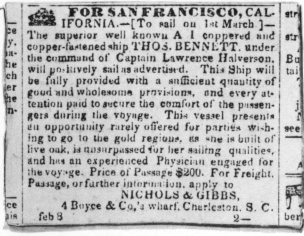

FOR SAN FRANCISCO, CALIFORNIA.—[To sail on 1st March.]—The superior well known A I coppered and copper-fastened ship THOS. BENNETT, under the command of Captain Lawrence Halverson, will positively sail as advertised. This Ship will be fully provided with a sufficient quantity of good and wholesome provisions, and every attention paid to secure the comfort of the passengers during the voyage. This vessel presents an opportunity rarely offered for parties wishing to go to the gold regions, as she is built of live oak, is unsurpassed for her sailing qualities, and has an experienced Physician engaged for the voyage. Price of Passage $200. For Freight, Passage, or further information, apply to
NICHOLS & GIBBS,
4 Boyce & Co,'s wharf, Charleston. S. C.
feb 8                                    2—

From the *Savannah Georgian*, Feb. 9, 1849.
*Courtesy*, Georgia Historical Society, Savannah, Ga.

# CALIFORNIA
## AGENCY OFFICE.

Persons who wish to secure a passage to California will do well to call on the subscriber, who has opened an office for the express accommodation of persons wishing to embark for the

## GOLD REGIONS.

He is employed by several Companies for the convenience of those wishing to secure passage. The ships are of the first class, being well victualled and ventilated, and commanded by experienced navigators.

Persons from the Country desiring information in regard to securing a passage can write to the subscriber by mail, at

**CLARKE'S**
GENERAL AGENCY OFFICE.
78 ANN STREET.
(A few doors from Blackstone Street.)
Life Insurance effected on the most advantageous terms and with surety.

Propeller Power Presses, 142 Washington St., Boston.

*Courtesy*, American Antiquarian Society, Worcester, Mass.

# FOR
# CALIFORNIA!
## Mutual Protection
## Trading & Mining Co.

Having purchased the splendid, Coppered and very fast Sailing

# Barque EMMA ISIDORA,

**Will leave about the 15th of February. This vessel will be fitted in the very best manner and is one of the fastest sailing vessels that goes from this port.**

Each member pays 300 dollars and is entitled to an equal proportion of all profits made by the company either at mining or trading, and holds an equal share of all the property belonging to the company. Experienced men well acquainted with the coast and climate are already engaged as officers of the Company. A rare chance is offered to any wishing a safe investment, good home and Large profits.

This Company is limited to 60 and any wishing to improve this opportunity must make immediate application.

An Experienced Physician will go with the company.

For Freight or Passage apply to 23 State Street, corner of Devonshire, where the list of Passengers may be seen.

## JAMES H. PRINCE, Agent,
### 23 State Street, corner of Devonshire St., Boston.

For further Particulars, see the Constitution.

Propeller Power Presses,
142 Washington St., Boston.

Henry Lewis, *Das Illustrirte Mississippithal.* 1854-57

The luxury of a sea voyage was denied the many families who were driven by poverty or restlessness to seek with bag, baggage and children this latest of promised lands.

For these, and most people departing from the interior states, the overland trails led to the golden country.

Down the rivers to the Mississippi by steamboat (*left*) and then up the Missouri to the jumping-off places—Kansas, Weston, St. Joseph, Council Bluffs—

—then over the great plains to the South Pass of the Rocky Mountains.

Or, by the way the returned soldiers from the War with Mexico preferred: the trail that the traders had broken to Santa Fe, and Kearny's route westward along the Gila River.

Either way, the wild loneliness of the prairies would swallow them up. But most of them knew the prairies only in pictures like the one *right*.

George Wilkins Kendall, *Narrative of the Texan Santa Fe Expedition.* 1844

THE OVERLAND ROUTE.

Alonzo Delano, *Life on the Plains and Among the Diggings.* 1854

On every overland trail the journey would be made in prairie wagons, their bodies built of well-seasoned lumber, caulked like a ship for fording the numberless streams. Oxen were best to draw them. Carry a rifle, knife and pistol—125 pounds of flour a man, 50 pounds of bacon—plenty of horse-shoe nails—be sure the tires could be loosened and tightened—take it easy on the plains—be ready for the Sierra—or the desert!

With a pathetic faith in the integrity of the printed word, the emigrants turned to guidebooks for light and leading through the wilderness.

Fremont's reports were reprinted again and again, and studied to tatters during that winter of 1848.

Books like that shown *right*, the work of a clever young man on his way, he hoped, to be ruler of Oregon and California, gave in addition to glowing descriptions of the goal, some "time-saving" variations of the route.

THE

# EMIGRANTS' GUIDE,

TO

## OREGON AND CALIFORNIA,

CONTAINING SCENES AND INCIDENTS OF A PARTY OF
OREGON EMIGRANTS;

### A DESCRIPTION OF OREGON;

SCENES AND INCIDENTS OF A PARTY OF CALIFORNIA
EMIGRANTS;

AND

## A DESCRIPTION OF CALIFORNIA;

WITH

A DESCRIPTION OF THE DIFFERENT ROUTES TO
THOSE COUNTRIES;

AND

ALL NECESSARY INFORMATION RELATIVE TO THE
EQUIPMENT, SUPPLIES, AND THE METHOD
OF TRAVELING.

BY LANSFORD W. HASTINGS,

Leader of the Oregon and California Emigrants of 1842.

CINCINNATI:
PUBLISHED BY GEORGE CONCLIN,
STEREOTYPED BY SHEPARD & CO.
1845.

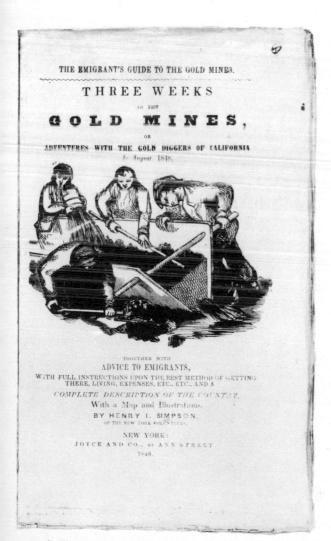

THE EMIGRANT'S GUIDE TO THE GOLD MINES.

# THREE WEEKS

IN THE

# GOLD MINES,

OR

ADVENTURES WITH THE GOLD DIGGERS OF CALIFORNIA

In August 1848.

TOGETHER WITH

ADVICE TO EMIGRANTS,

WITH FULL INSTRUCTIONS UPON THE BEST METHOD OF GETTING
THERE, LIVING, EXPENSES, ETC., ETC., AND A

*COMPLETE DESCRIPTION OF THE COUNTRY.*

With a Map and Illustrations.

BY HENRY I. SIMPSON,
OF THE NEW YORK VOLUNTEERS.

NEW YORK:
JOYCE AND CO., 49 ANN STREET.
1848.

There was a little too much cleverness about in those days. Hastings was clever; Henry I. Simpson (*left*) was clever; a pity they could not have been a little more critical. For these were but a sample of many such misleading documents which fed the excitement and sent trusting and incapable folk after an impossible dream by ways that existed largely in the imagination.

Both illustrations on this page are by the *courtesy* of The Bancroft Library, University of California, Berkeley, Calif.

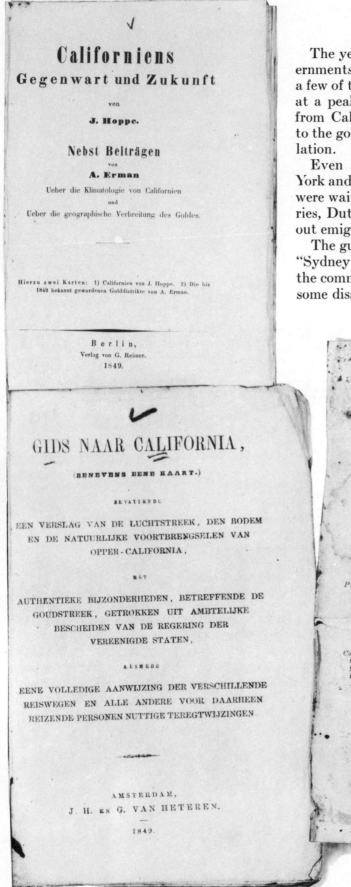

The year 1848 had been a difficult time for the governments of Europe. Revolutions had shaken all but a few of the Old World states, and unemployment was at a peak. European statesmen looked on the news from California as an answer to prayer. Emigration to the gold fields would take care of the surplus population.

Even as the prospective gold-seekers from New York and New England, from Ohio, Missouri, Indiana, were waiting for the spring grass to come on the prairies, Dutch and German presses were busily turning out emigration propaganda (*left*).

The guidebook shown *below* must have set many a "Sydney Duck" on the wing from the Antipodes. Note the comment pencilled in over the author's initials by some dissatisfied customer.

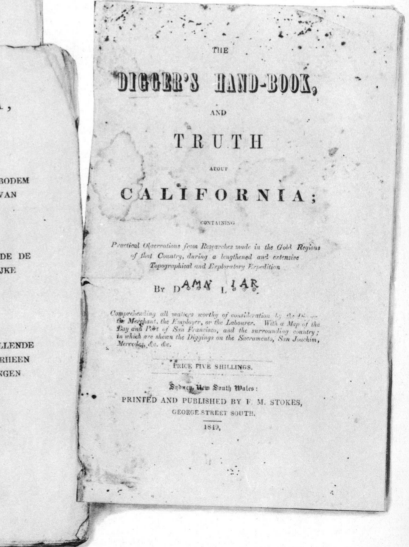

Most Frenchmen thought of America in terms of Cooper's novels or as in the illustration of a buffalo hunt shown *right*. But if discontented French citizens could find fortune at such a comfortable distance from home, then subscription to stock in the many "emigration aid societies" was as much a patriotic gesture and good social insurance as it might be a source of personal profit.

*La Fortune* company, one of whose advertisements is shown *below*, was gambling on the virtues of a patented "mining machine."

J. B. J. Champagnac, *Le Jeune Voyageur en Californie,* 1852

*Le Charivari,* June 25, 1850

One of Mr. Nathaniel Currier's artists suggested this air-line method of transportation to California. What appears to be an early jet-propelled model may be seen at the upper *left*.

LINE RAILWAY TO CALIFORNIA.

*Courtesy*, The New-York Historical Society, New York City

# 3

# They Saw the Elephant

TODAY WE CALL them Kansas City, Missouri, and Council Bluffs, Iowa. In the spring of 1849, they were Westport Landing and Kanesville, and at every likely spot along the Missouri River for some two hundred miles between them camped the restless men and women who were off to California by the northern overland route.

At night, in their tents and wagons they talked, formed "companies," chose officers, visited about, sang psalms and "Oh Susannah." By day they waited for the grass to grow, and snapped up every bit of gossip about what lay before them. Did you have cholera aboard your boat? We lost ten people. How much did you pay for your outfit? Captain Fremont says. . . .

Some of the emigrants had bought their food and their wagons, teams and yokes of cattle, back in St. Louis; others made the best bargains they could with the outfitters at Kansas and St. Joe and Kanesville. You took what was offered you; for speed was essential. The man who bought his trail equipment while you were shopping or making up your mind could very well best you in the race for fortune—the great, sporting lottery in which the prizes would go to the canny and the strong.

They were young men and women, those first rushers after the gold, but some middle-aged folk were among them still following the trail of the rainbow. They were educated folk, church-going and law-abiding as a rule, anxious that law and order should mark the great adventure. Their household goods were with them—stoves and harps and four-poster beds—despite all the warnings against heavy wagons and surplus equipment.

Deprived of her steamboat landing by one of the Missouri River's many whims, the town of Independence (*below*) had lost her primacy as a jumping-off place to the West. But dance halls and saloons and gambling tables operated there. Some emigrants saw no more of "the Elephant" than Independence, where money for oxen was lost on the turn of a card, and the liquor was strong.

Charles A. Dana, *The United States Illustrated.* 1853

Westport Landing (*right*) was a favorite starting point for the "companies" who came by river boats to take the California Trail. And many an emigrant camped at Weston (*below*), a Missouri village about opposite Fort Leavenworth. One of the officers of the Mounted Rifle Regiment made this sketch in 1849 before he left the Fort for the long, unfortunate march of the regiment to Oregon.

*Courtesy,* Stokes Collection, The New York Public Library

*Courtesy,* Wisconsin State Historical Society, Madison, Wis.

J. Goldsborough Bruff, the able, if sententious, Captain of the "Washington City and California Mining Association," showed his brass-buttoned splendor briefly at Weston before landing at St. Joe. His company went to work breaking mules and fitting-up at the camp shown *below,* two miles back of town at Blacksnake Hill. Bruff noted in his diary that there had been much talk of cholera on the river.

*Courtesy,* The Huntington Library, San Marino, Calif.

In April, 1847, Brigham Young had taken his first overland party of Mormons to the promised land of Deseret. Where they had crossed the Missouri, a ferry was running prosperously in 1849 (*left*). Many of the emigrants from the northern states crossed by it from Kanesville to what is now Omaha, Nebraska, and thereafter converged on the Platte.

At Kanesville (*below*), the Mormons drove a thriving trade in guidebooks: crudely printed leaves sewn together which promised "good water here—wood to the left—good grass." All of it might have been true the previous year.

Both illustrations on this page are from James Linforth, ed., *Route from Liverpool to Great Salt Lake Valley.* 1855. *Courtesy,* The New-York Historical Society, New York City

All the gold-seekers came together near the Grand Island, where Fort Childs, soon to be called Fort Kearny, was building on the banks of the Platte. But before the watcher at the Fort could add your outfit to the count he kept of westward-faring wagons, you had had to come up from Westport Landing or St. Joe, or straight across from what is now called Nebraska City, over the gently-rising, open prairie and the easily forded rivers and creeks that trenched the plains.

So long as the wideness of the sky, the flowers springing up in the grass, the bright, strange birds and the ground squirrels were new things and exciting, there was about the first stage of the trail something of a picnic, a grand, gay procession to El Dorado. The children laughed and ran about; the teams pulled with a will and you were tempted to overdrive them; sick and ailing folk began to perk up and cease their complaining.

A few pioneer farms were scattered along the road, to remind you of home and to give point to the lonesome songs that were sung of nights in the tents and the wagons. A passing soldier made the sketch *below* in 1849.

*Courtesy,* Wisconsin State Historical Society, Madison, Wis.

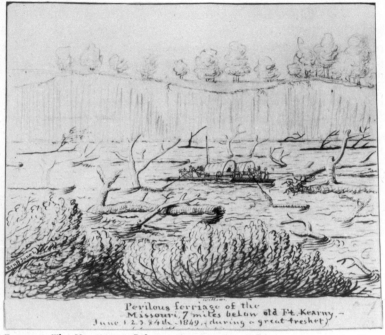

Captain Bruff and his Washington Company crossed the Missouri some seven miles below Nebraska City. At the *left* is the sketch he made in June, 1849, as his wagons were being ferried over through the drift of the usual flood.

*Perilous ferriage of the Missouri, 7 miles below old Ft. Kearny.—June 1 2. 3. & 4th -1849. (during a great freshet)*

*Courtesy*, The Huntington Library, San Marino, Calif.

The sketch *below* shows how the wagons of another outfit were let down the banks of some prairie river; probably the Nemeha or the Big Blue.

*Courtesy*, Wisconsin State Historical Society, Madison, Wis.

The road from Kanesville along the northern bank of the Platte crossed many streams, small and large, before reaching that point opposite Grand Island where the emigrants could see across the river the wagon trains coming up to the "coasts of the Platte" from Westport and St. Joe. The view *above* shows wagons at the Elk Horn River ferry on the Mormon Trail. *Below* is shown the ferry across the Loup Fork.

Both illustrations on this page are from James Linforth, ed., *Route from Liverpool to Great Salt Lake Valley*. 1855. *Courtesy*, The New-York Historical Society, New York City

James Linforth, ed., *Route from Liverpool to Great Salt Lake Valley*. 1855.
*Courtesy*, The New-York Historical Society, New York City

Few camps were as orderly as the one at Wood River *above*. The wagons are neatly arranged in corral; the oxen appear satisfied amid plenty of good grass. Once you were past Pawnee country, there was no particular danger from Indians (though the fear of them rode with you always); the principal danger lay in the subtle pressure of sun and dust and sky upon the nerves; the sickness incident to a diet of "hog and hominy" only slightly varied by an occasional taste of raccoon, or wild onions; the dreaded cholera of that year; and the dysentery brought on by drinking the waters of mineral springs. Sometimes at night there was a grand illumination; the prairie grass would flame up in an ever-widening semi-circle of fire.

From a painting by George Winter. *Courtesy*, The William Henry Smith Memorial Library of The Indiana Historical Society, Indianapolis, Ind.

Grass-covered sand-hills bordered the valley of the Platte as you moved toward Fort Childs. The valley itself was level as a floor and through it flowed the mile-wide, muddy river with Grand Island threading down its middle. Moving westward along the river, or encamped in the bottoms, were the gold-seekers, united at last in one striving multitude. When Alonzo Delano, nineteen days out from the Missouri, first saw the long line of trains in motion he noted: "We could scarcely realize that we were in an Indian country from the scene of civilized life before us; and this was all caused by the magic talisman of gold! What will be the end? Who can foresee our future destiny?" And he went on, with less of oratory, "We felt a great change in the atmosphere. From being warm it became so cold that overcoats were necessary for comfort."

At the Fort itself, there was only a cluster of one-story, adobe barracks, surrounded by a wall still in process of construction. Small comfort there! Wood was scarce for fires. Small willow branches and buffalo chips were the best you could do. And winds and torrential rainstorms began to beat down on the emigrants as the trail moved on from the Fort toward the Forks, where the river divided into the North and South Platte. Water drove in through tent flaps and wagon-covers; by day the skies were overcast "with the gloom and air of November rather than the genial warmth of spring." The cattle would not drink the river water; under the pelting rain they broke from the corral or from their tethers and wandered away.

The great adventure had ceased to be fun. All along the way, you began to notice the bits of plank that stood up from cleared spots beside the road—headstones of a sort over new-made graves.

At the crossing of the South Platte (*below*), the bottom was treacherous and the current brisk. Teams were doubled and no time was lost in fording the river.

*Courtesy,* Wisconsin State Historical Society, Madison, Wis.

The Indians of the plains wrapped their dead in a blanket and buffalo skin and raised him up on a platform, out of the reach of the wolves. With him they put his cup and his moccasins and all the things he might need in the spirit world. Delano saw some of these graves as his train neared Ash Hollow where the trail touched the North Platte after the ford of the south branch. "Some Goths from Missouri wantonly cut the limbs away and let the body fall."

Buffalo now began to appear in large numbers. The emigrants often came to grief in hunting them, for a buffalo wounded or hard-pressed would turn and charge.

Both illustrations on this page are from H. R. Schoolcraft, *Information respecting Indian Tribes of the U. S. 1851-57*

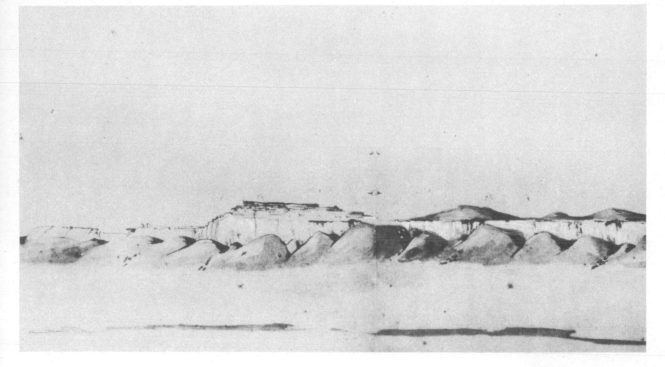

*Courtesy,* Wisconsin State Historical Society, Madison, Wis.

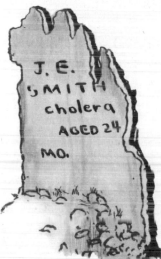

Those gold-seekers who had been driving their cattle hard began to appreciate the warnings they had been given back in Missouri. The cattle began to go lame and to give out. Along the trail, under the fantastic line of cliffs, were scattered trunks and iron stoves; piles of bacon; bags of coffee; broken wagons; sugar on which turpentine had been poured lest any succeeding emigrant should use it; clothing torn to ribbons so that it could not be worn.

The limitless horizon narrowed. Walls of hard clayey rock (*above*) rose up and bounded the bottoms of the North Platte. Conspicuous among the landmarks were "Court House Rock" and "Jail Rock" (*below*).

James Truslow Adams, ed., *Album of American History.* 1945

James Linforth, ed., *Route from Liverpool to Great Salt Lake Valley.* 1855.
*Courtesy,* The New-York Historical Society, New York City

By Chimney Rock (*above*), the dust, driven by the everlasting wind of the plains, cut into your flesh; the cattle labored hard on the sandy trail. Water holes and wells yielded only a turbid liquid the color of lye, and the ground about them was whitened as with frost. The cliffs assumed all manner of shapes; sometimes like ancient castles, sometimes like giant, man-made walls, and in the clear air seemed to overhang the trail.

The mean streak hidden in many a man came out when the teams were put to Mitchell's Pass through Scotts Bluff (*below*). Here, grass and water were alike poor, and at the western extremity of the Pass the country grew barren and dull.

James Truslow Adams, ed., *Album of American History.* 1945

*Courtesy*, Wisconsin State Historical Society, Madison, Wis.

The trail between Scotts Bluff and Fort Laramie was not particularly difficult, but irritation with tiny things became more acute—a man's moustache, his smell, the way he wore his hat, ground inward on you and you almost hated him. At Laramie Creek (*above*), the current was swift and chancy. Wagons capsized in the stream. Water flooded in on the provisions.

Though the picture *below*, made by one who passed Fort Laramie in 1849, shows the Fort in good order, most of the emigrants commented on the dilapidated condition of the adobe walls, supported by long, wooden props.

From this point on, the trail left the plains and entered the mountainous country. The next point where supplies could be procured would be Fort Bridger, three hundred and ninety-odd miles away.

*U. S. Senate, Executive Document No. 1, 31st Congress, 2nd Session*

T. GREEN
or CHOL-
ERA
20 JUNE '49

When you passed Laramie Peak (*above*) you were aware of the change in the trail—the transition from the dusty plains to the newer air and the newer dangers. If cholera and dysentery declined, "mountain fever" took their places.

Now the trail was all up and down in the rugged nakedness of the Black Hills (*below*), later known as the Laramie Mountains.

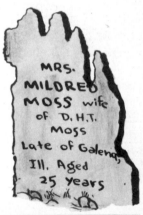

MRS.
MILDRED
MOSS wife
of D. H. T.
MOSS
Late of Galena,
Ill. Aged
25 years

Both illustrations on this page are by the *courtesy* of the Wisconsin State Historical Society, Madison, Wis.

*Courtesy,* Wisconsin State Historical Society, Madison, Wis.

Lips cracked, faces burnt red by sun and alkali, hair long and uncombed, coats greasy and tattered, feeding out of the pork barrel, the emigrants pressed on through the Black Hills (*above*). "Drive on, Hazel. Ho! for California."

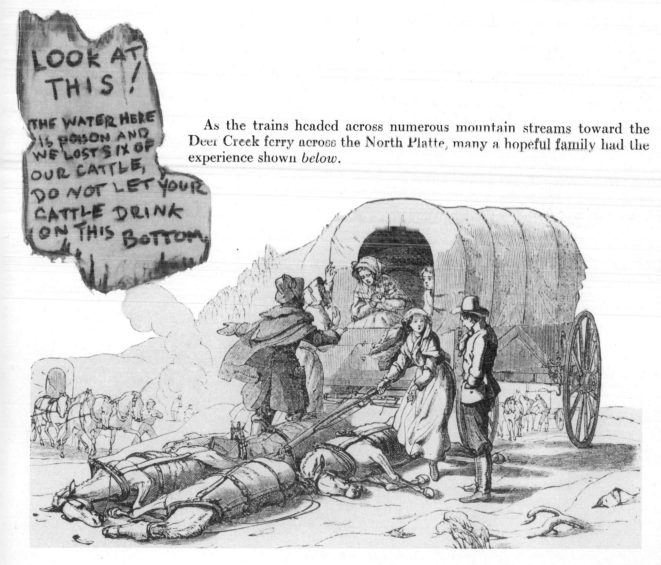

As the trains headed across numerous mountain streams toward the Deer Creek ferry across the North Platte, many a hopeful family had the experience shown *below*.

Alonzo Delano, *Old Block's Sketch-Book; or, Tales of California Life.* 1856

Howard Stansbury, *Exploration and Survey of the Valley of the Great Salt Lake of Utah.* 1852

After making the north shore of the river on the primitive ferry shown *above*, the trail left the Platte and crossed the barren ground, amid sagebrush and prickly pear bushes, in thirst and weariness, that lay between the Platte and the Sweetwater Rivers. It was intensely hot. Carcasses of dead cattle were numerous. Worn-out, abandoned animals wandered about, shifting for themselves.

Then suddenly, when any water would have been welcome, you stumbled over the Sweetwater, eighty feet wide, a running stream that by comparison with the muddy and insipid Platte seemed like the veritable waters of salvation. At the crossing, standing up lonely in the undulating plain, was Independence Rock (*below*), its walls carved and painted with the names of those who had passed that way before you.

James Linforth, ed., *Route from Liverpool to Great Salt Lake Valley.* 1855.
*Courtesy,* The New-York Historical Society, New York City

Water and pasturage were good in the valley of the Sweetwater. Herds of buffalo and antelope grazed there. Once through the grim cleft of Devil's Gate (*right*) the river flowed placidly along, and the trail meandered beside it and across it.

James Linforth, ed., *Route from Liverpool to Great Salt Lake Valley,* 1855. *Courtesy,* The New-York Historical Society, New York City

From an occasional elevation in the floor of the valley, the emigrants could see the loom of the mountains.

*Courtesy,* Wisconsin State Historical Society, Madison, Wis.

At the end of a weary day, after crossing the winding Sweetwater again and again through deep and bad fords, the tents had to be pitched, the cattle driven out to graze wherever grass might be, and guards stationed to see that they did not stray or drink poisoned water. Buffalo chips had to be gathered for fuel; what food there might be had to be cooked. Then came the uncertain night. Even after weeks on the trail, sentries mistook shadows and prowling small animals for Indians and bears; alarm shots were fired; the encampment would be in an uproar. Tempers strained and broke. Men shot one another and could give only trivial reasons.

There were many strange things on this long, slow ascent to the South Pass through the Rocky Mountains. When you dug for a foot or so under a surface of wild grass on the border of a swamp, you struck not water but ice, the remnant of a previous wild winter when the morass had been frozen solid. Tributary streams to the Sweetwater showed golden-gleaming specks and scales in their beds. Gold! Here where so many had already passed! But out came the little bottle of nitric acid and the dreams dissolved. Fool's gold! And in this desolate place, fit only for a passage to fortune, some white men lived. They came down from the mountains with their Indian wives and half-breed children to stand beside the trail and trade with the emigrants.

For days, many carcasses had been littering the road—mules, oxen, worn-out by overexertion in the thin, mountain air. The trail was mounting higher and higher but imperceptibly, slowly and treacherously. You could tell it in the way your chest ached and your feet dragged. A final ford of the Sweetwater up near its source, and then a level road for almost eight miles to the South Pass!

It was not much to look at—no sharp decisive cut through a wall of rock—only a broad, level way between conical hills or knolls and then a descent to the first water which flows westerly from the crest, Pacific Springs (*below*). To the north, over a broken mountain plain lay the Wind River Mountains, snow-capped and grand.

*Courtesy*, Wisconsin State Historical Society, Madison, Wis.

Two principal ways there were to the valley of the Bear River, up which the California Trail marched almost to Fort Hall on the Snake. One way went by Fort Bridger, where old Jim had set up a trading station on Black's Fork of the Green River in the winter of '43. "It promises fairly," he wrote that year, "They (*the emigrants*) in coming out are generally well supplied with money, but by the time they get here are in want of all kinds of supplies."

If you went by way of Fort Bridger, you could refit there for the drive to Bear River valley and the wells of the Humboldt. Or at Bridger, you might change your mind and decide to head for Salt Lake City. Thence you might

*Courtesy,* Wisconsin State Historical Society, Madison, Wis.

take Hastings' road to the Humboldt, or follow the Spanish Trail to Los Angeles.

To get to Fort Bridger from Pacific Springs, you had to ford the Green River near the mouth of its tributary, the Big Sandy (*above*).

This journey from South Pass to Green River was made through a barren, sandy waste. In summer, the heat and dust were almost too much after all that you had been through.

Once across the ford, the road crossed over to Black's Fork. Thirty seven miles further you came to a mountain stream, icy from the crests of the Uintas and alive with trout. Beside it was Fort Bridger (*below*).

MARGARET CAMPBELL departed July 28, 1848 Aged 36 yrs, 4 Mos 23 days

Howard Stansbury, *Exploration and Survey of the Valley of the Great Salt Lake of Utah.* 1852

*Courtesy*, The Huntington Library, San Marino, Calif.

The alternate route to Bear River, which cut off from the main road beyond Pacific Springs and drove across a waterless desert for almost sixty miles, descended to the Green River valley down a rubble of clay, loose stones and bits of slate near the mouth of Labarge Creek, as shown *above* in one of J. G. Bruff's drawings. But whether you went by this way or by way of Fort Bridger, you came at last to the intricate series of ravines and valleys through which the Bear River flowed to the north. "The descent of these hills was sometimes precipitous," wrote one of the emigrants. For all its ups and downs (see *below*), the valley of the Bear was the best route to Fort Hall and the wells of the Humboldt.

*Courtesy*, Wisconsin State Historical Society, Madison, Wis.

As the trains wound up the Bear River valley, the gold-hunters were astonished to find conical mounds on either side of the river which huffed and puffed and spouted pure soda water. These little previews of what the Yellowstone was later to reveal on a grand scale were called "Beer Springs" (*above*) and "Steamboat Springs" (*below*). About three miles further on, the trail followed a dry valley to a point south of Fort Hall.

Most of the emigrants commented on the change in the physical appearance of the Indians, once the Rockies had been crossed. The Snakes and Paiutes who lived in the Bear, Raft and Humboldt River regions seemed less majestic and impressive than the Indians of the Plains, but experience was to show that they were supremely gifted as sneak thieves.

Both illustrations on this page are by the *courtesy* of the Wisconsin State Historical Society, Madison, Wis.

They still could sing. In spite of the weariness and the dirt; the sometimes violent breakup of those companies and trail organizations of which they had been so proud; the slow increase of lawlessness as sickness and death stalked the trains; they could gather in camp near the Fort and entertain the traders and squaws with banjo and accordion, with "Zip Coon," "Old Dan Tucker" and "Carry Me Back To Old Virginny."

Fort Hall was out of the way to California and fortune; the air was loud with praises of the wonderful new cut-off direct from Beer Springs to the head of Raft River; yet many emigrants felt they could spare time to rest weary legs and look at some new faces. Many cattle had died. Many surviving animals were so weakened that their masters were making the journey virtually on foot to save the beasts for that part of the California Trail to come—the last and hardest trial of the great adventure. Slowly, the Elephant of legend, the thing they went out to see, the subject of all those jokes back home in Louisville, or Galena, or St. Louis, was becoming in many minds a symbol of that great rock wall ahead of them, the Sierra Nevada.

The Fort was a disappointment. It was smaller than Laramie and more dilapidated; a mere fur-trading station on the edge of a desert, a discouraging sight after the lovely valley of Bear River. But letters were written and posted there; clothing was washed and mended; a few supplies were bought; and at last the teams were headed again westward.

A burning sun and endless clouds of dust as you traveled down the valley of the sluggish River Snake; more sun and more dust on the desert drive to the thin thread of water meandering in the desert which was called Raft River. All the strange ways to the golden country came together at some point on that little stream: Hudspeth's illusory cut-off; the road up from Salt Lake City; the road down from Fort Hall. On either side of the bottom lands, tall hills rose abruptly and you found them made of that flinty rock, hard and bleak and seemingly still glistening with the light of the volcanic fires that made them, which would grow increasingly terrible as the trail marched down the Humboldt River toward the Sierra passes. It was hot. Many of the unfortunates who had been stranded before your outfit came along, stood alongside the trail and begged for clothing, for food, for a lift. It was hard to refuse; harder to give when you knew what was still ahead and had so little for yourself.

When you came to Goose Creek valley on your way to the wells of the Humboldt, your mind was prepared by weeks of anxiety, alkali dust and misfortune to find an eerie quality in the columns and minarets of volcanic rock. And it was there you saw, amid what Delano called "the breaking up of the world," the breaking up of many men's hopes. Where the trail led down a steep cliff, almost sheer, and the descent had to be made by ropes—wagons, ironware, household goods were scattered about derelict. The owners had saddled the failing mules, killed the cattle for food and driven ahead desperately.

The wells of the Humboldt gave rise to a strange and unsatisfactory river, none too full, none too sweet, hemmed in by high and barren mountains from whose flanks rose slender smoke columns to show that the thieving Digger Indians were watching for a chance to raid and steal the animals that stood between you and death in a desert. The trail ran, sometimes along the banks near good grass, sometimes high up on naked spurs. There were no trees. The sun beat down, the dust was blown in your face by the constant west wind; always the dust in your food, in your drink, chafing your skin. It was best to travel by night when others were asleep and the restless wheels ahead were not churning up the trail. There were almost three hundred miles of it; from the source of the Humboldt to Lassen's Meadows.

*U. S. Senate, Executive Document No. 1, 31st Congress, 2nd Session*

Fort Hall *above.*

Near the basalt columns in Goose Creek valley shown *below*, Captain Bruff saw and copied the following notice, stuck in a cleft stick:

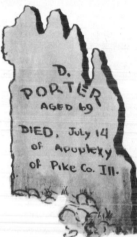

---

### PUBLIC SALE

*Will be sold on Sunday, 2d Sept., on the head of Mary's River, Stores and a lot of merchandise. Emigrants in the rear will do well to be there, as great bargains will be sold.*

---

*Courtesy,* California Historical Society, San Francisco, Calif.

The Valley of the Humboldt River (*above*); Lassen's Meadows at left.

The network of valleys and ravines alongside the fast-diminishing Humboldt River made no sense; it ran here and there without rhyme or reason. Sometimes the bed of the river was almost dry, or a mere series of pools, strongly alkaline. The overhanging mountains seemed jumbled together on the ashy plain.

Rumors began to drift back along the line of wagons: there was no grass at the Sink of the Humboldt, the place where the river died in desert sands. And you began to hear of a desert, forty miles and more without water, that lay beyond the Sink and ran to the foot of the mountain wall. To those who had seen fail them, first wagon teams, then riding mules, and who were now pressing along on foot under heavy packs, this was sad news. Men clutched at straws; many of them followed a new road which was said to avoid the desert by a northern passage of the Sierra.

The water holes were not to be trusted. Abandoned cattle died while drinking at them, fell in and polluted the water unless the wolves pulled out the carcasses. But after the river turned southwest beyond its big bend, there was something to be thankful for. The long, lush, grass valley called Lassen's Meadows lay right in the path; better than a thousand acres of grazing for the dead-beat cattle—and water—blessed water—in the parched and burning valley! Every cask, keg and bucket was filled in preparation for a hundred miles of hell before you could come through Carson Canyon, over the roof of the Sierra, to El Dorado.

U. S. House of Representatives, Executive Document No. 91, 33rd Congress, 2nd Session

Five miles west of the end of the Sink was the head of that dry region called Humboldt Lake and below those desolate miles was Humboldt Slough where you had your last chance at water before you made the run for the Carson River across Carson Sink and the desert divide between the Humboldt and the Carson Valleys.

*Every morning in California, the dew settles on the petals of acres of roses, to become hard and candied like a sweet and heavenly manna!*

Heat and dust! And yet any delay would lead to a worse peril—the crossing of the mountains in late fall or winter! You had to push on to the Sink; to the morass of Humboldt Slough, the animals sinking almost belly-deep in the ashy sand. The stink of putrid carcasses hung over the route; and miles of desert lay ahead before you came to Carson Valley. It was not always the cattle that died.

*Gold! Gold on the American River! You scratch the earth and there she is. Big, yellow chunks!*

The Valley of the Humboldt River (*above*): from Lassen's Meadows (*right*) to the Sink (extreme *left*).

The sand piled up in hills and dunes on the desert. You had checked your outfit at the Slough —taken the wheels off the wagon and soaked them—checked tongues, axles, harness—replaced worn and broken parts with others taken from the many wagons that lay abandoned by the trail. Even here in the shadow of death, the meanness of some men showed itself in attempts made to burn or destroy what could serve them no longer and might aid other men to win the golden goal.

At the Desert Wells, beyond the Carson Sink, the water was bad. You had to dig down in the shallow holes before it seeped up. But it was the one spot between Humboldt Slough and the Carson River where there was water at all. Many of the wagons had notches cut in the tailboards, where grave markers had been cut. There were stories told of outfits which missed the chance for water at Lassen's Meadows, fared out on the desert far up and never were heard of again. There were stories of men who went insane on this last stretch of the trail and came to the Carson River, trussed up like animals in their own wagons. It was near the Desert Wells that the alternate route to California through Truckee Pass branched off from the trail.

*U. S. House of Representatives, Executive Document No. 91, 33rd Congress, 2nd Session*

All the way along the final stretch, the animals were mad for water. They could scent it from afar, they could hear it dipped or poured from a canteen. They stampeded and were unmanageable.

Not the animals only rushed down the sloping ground at first sight of the ribbon of green that marked the Carson River's course. Men and women threw themselves down and sucked up the water greedily, wallowed in it, surfeited themselves.

At the Carson River was another great deposit of wagons, ironware, feather-beds, wagon-covers, furniture; the witness of who knows what trouble and what hopes, what dreams and what disappointments. Ragtown was the name given that first station on the Carson River. A vast junkshop, with the wind blowing the lighter stuff along the shore and the plain, and a trader's tent where the only commodity was whisky at twenty five cents a drink!

After the forty-mile desert drive, the eighty-odd miles under the cottonwoods that fringed the Carson River were comparatively easy. Now and again a finger of desert touched the trail to remind you of perils past. But at last you came to the ledges in Carson Canyon (*above*) where the road leapt up to the frowning summits that lay between you and the gold. At the western end of Red Lake (*below*), you faced the first and lesser summit of the Sierra. Here, where those who had preceded you had shouldered up the road with logs so that wagons might climb it, the very rocks seemed to fight against you as the road twisted around the edge of profound and echoing chasms.

*Courtesy,* California Historical Society, San Francisco, Calif.

Once over the first summit, you rested the animals amid the scrub pine trees and the snow drifts. The second, western ridge had still to be scaled by a road that dipped sideways in places and was almost incredibly steep. But after you had climbed and cursed your way to the crest of the mountain wall *above,* you looked down on the rivers and valleys you had come so far to see—the Sacramento and the San Joaquin, with all their golden tributaries. Over steep grades and sandy, you descended to California. There were men in those days.

These views of Carson Canyon, Red Lake, and the second summit of the Sierra Nevada were sketched from daguerreotypes made in 1851 by J. Wesley Jones (and now lost), whose desire to write and lecture about the grand phenomenon of a nation on the march took him out on the California Trail and supplied what are possibly the only contemporary pictures of these subjects in existence.

An emigrant who cut off from the trail at the Desert Wells and headed for California by way of Truckee River (*right*) and one of the alternate passes across the Sierra to Yuba River may be allowed to speak for himself:

"The great desert from the Sink to Truckee River was an awful place. The water at the warm springs in the center was poisonous to all kinds of stock, and the road on the desert was lined with dead cattle, mules and horses, with here and there a wagon . . . we left no cattle there, but several gave out and laid down when within about six miles of Truckee . . . The road from and up the Truckee River to the Summit was bad, but the road from the Summit to Johnson's settlement is the most damnable road on the face of the earth . . ."

Near the summit of the Sierra Nevada, one of the Truckee River routes passed the lake shown *below*. About this spot still hung the horror and the memory of the Donner group of emigrants who had camped nearby in the winter of 1846. It was here they had waited for spring, and eaten their dead comrades as the snow rose higher and higher.

Both illustrations on this page are modern and are used by the *courtesy* of the Southern Pacific Company, San Francisco, Calif.

Hangtown Cal

*Courtesy*, California Historical Society, San Francisco, Calif.

For those who came gaily down the slopes on the western side of the Sierra, singing, rejoicing; wagon-wheels screaming under brakes, stock fat and saucy again; there were four days of rough travel before they saw Hangtown (*above*)—the shantytown outpost of El Dorado—the end of twenty-two hundred miles of labor and suffering—where she sat like a squalid queen beside one of the creeks of the American River.

The first gold-rushers of 1848 had called the place Old Dry Diggings. Perry McCoon and William Daylor had taken time off from their farms on the Cosumnes and prospected west of Coloma. In their first week along the creek at what was to be Hangtown they had taken out seventeen thousand dollars worth of gold dust and started a rush to the place.

The first recorded executions for murder in all the gold region had been performed there in January, 1849, and given Old Dry Diggings a new name. Hangtown it was, but it would not remain so. Log houses replaced tents and wickiups. The "pan" miners moved on, but wiser heads found that a cradle worked very well with the gravel from Hangtown Creek. The town aspired; grew genteel in its way; disliked the associations of its old name.

J. M. Letts, *A Pictorial View of California.* 1853

When J. M. Letts made the sketch *left,* Hangtown had already become Placerville.

There was still room for improvement, however. To enter the Yankee's House at Placerville, you had to crawl in and double up like a jackknife.

J. M. Letts, *A Pictorial View of California.* 1853

Many an exhausted gold-seeker, stumbling down into the Sacramento Valley without food or outfit, found generous aid at Sutter's Fort, seen at the *left* as it appeared in 1849.

Rescue parties of Sutter's employees went out eastward on the trail to bring help to emigrants stranded in the passes.

# 4

# Easier Roads to Fortune

## THE LASSEN ROAD

RUMOR HAD ten thousand tongues along the trail to California. "No grass at the Sink of the Humboldt—no water at the desert wells—early snow falling in the mountain passes!" The weary men and women listened to tales of alternative routes, guaranteed to flow with milk and honey—tales of low, easy passes through the northern ranges of the Sierra.

By the time the earliest gold-seekers had endured the first two hundred miles along the Humboldt—the dust, the Indian raids—the death of stock, friends and almost the death of hope—they gave eager ear to the talk of a "new" road: Lassen's Road named for a pioneer who in 1844 had built the first civilized habitation north of Marysville. It branched off beyond the big bend southward that the Humboldt River made, and pointed northwest across Black Rock Desert, through Cedar Pass or Lassen Pass and struck into the valley of Pit River. Some authorities claim that almost half the gold-seekers of '49 were deceived into going this way and exchanging forty miles of Carson Desert for one hundred miles of grimmer waste country.

What was left of the Washington City "Company" yielded to Captain Bruff's persuasive oratory and chose this route. After thirty-five miles of deep sand and sagebrush, hardly able to crawl for thirst and fatigue, they came to water—Rabbit Hole Springs (below).

*Courtesy*, The Huntington Library, San Marino, Calif.

Bruff's confidence in the new road began to wane, but it was too late to turn back. The Washington City Company pushed on across the desert of alkali. Mirages bewildered the men with visions of long, blue lagoons, bordered by shade trees. After thirteen days of this, Bruff and his men crossed the Sierra and began to descend the valley of Pit River. In the background of the picture *above* is Fremont's "Round Valley" where Lassen's Road joined the route from Oregon to California.

The hostility of the Pit River Indians, the worn-out condition of the mules, and the approach of winter, all influenced Bruff to stay with the wagons in winter quarters (*below*), while his men pushed ahead to the mines.

Belated gold-seekers, hurrying down the Sacramento Valley, found in Bruff a kind friend. The ungrateful members of his Company, however, after returning from Lassen's Ranch to claim their property, informed him they wanted no more to do with him.

Unable to buy a team, disgusted, rheumatic, and shocked by the selfishness of emigrants who refused him a lift, Bruff decided to stay in the deserted winter quarters until spring. After a terrible siege of hunger and sickness, the monotony of snow varied only by incidents like that sketched *above*, living on such delicacies as acorns, old deer-legs and the frozen remains of long-deceased oxen, Bruff stumbled down the thirty-two miles to Lassen's Ranch (*below*) near the mouth of Deer Creek.

Both illustrations on this page are by the *courtesy* of The Huntington Library, San Marino, Calif.

# THE SALT LAKE-LOS ANGELES ROAD

Rumors about Humboldt Valley had caused many emigrants to seek a better route, long before coming to Lassen's Road. At Fort Bridger, a road branched left to Salt Lake City. From there they could get to southern California along a well-marked trail.

They approached the Mormon capital from the east by way of Weber River valley (*above*). "Good grass, wood and water," said the guidebooks.

The mountain barrier opened at last and revealed the Great Salt Lake to the eager watchers (*below*).

Both illustrations on this page are from Howard Stansbury, *Exploration and Survey of the Valley of the Great Salt Lake of Utah.* 1852

*Howard Stansbury, Exploration and Survey of the Valley of the Great Salt Lake of Utah. 1852*

Streets in Salt Lake City (*above*) were laid out according to an ideal plan for the City of Zion, prepared by Joseph Smith in 1833. Though only two years old, the town was flourishing in 1849; saplings had been planted; plentiful water brought from the mountains; gardens were everywhere. It was a pleasant place to refit and consider the future.

Some of the gold-seekers were foolish enough to follow Hastings' Road from Salt Lake City across the Salt Desert, past the ox-skeletons and ruined wagons left by the Donner group in 1846. Ninety miles of desert—and then by a pass as rugged as that shown *below* they came down on the parched valley of the Humboldt, with Carson Desert still to cross!

*U. S. House of Representatives. Executive Document No. 91, 33rd Congress, 2nd Session*

But the best way from Salt Lake City to California was the Mormon caravan trail which ran east of Utah Lake (*above*) through the southern Mormon settlements to the valley of the Sevier River. It paralleled and then joined the Old Spanish Trail from Santa Fe to Los Angeles, following the valley of the Virgin River (*below*) until that river bent southward.

Both illustrations on this page (drawn eighteen years later by W. H. Jackson), are by the *courtesy* of the National Park Service, U. S. Department of the Interior.

Three hundred miles of desert lay beyond the troublesome valley of the Virgin. The hot and dusty journey was broken at occasional springs of bitter water (*above*, Cottonwood Springs), but the best part of the way lay over the Mohave Desert (*below*), between the tall spikes of the yuccas.

Both illustrations on this page are by the *courtesy* of the National Park Service, U. S. Department of the Interior

At the western end of the Mohave Desert, the trail climbed the Coast Range by way of Cajon Pass (*left*), and the emigrants made fairly easy time down the western slopes to Rancho San Bernardino, and to Los Angeles.

From Los Angeles (*below*, as it looked *circa* 1853) the gold-seekers traveled northward to the mines. They might go overland, or after traveling some thirty miles from the Pueblo to the coast, they might get passage by ship to San Francisco.

Both illustrations on this page are from *Senate Executive Document No. 78, 33rd Congress, 2nd Session*

# DEATH VALLEY

Some few attempted a short route to the gold regions which was said to lead by way of Walker's Pass to the southern mines. It turned off the Salt Lake-Los Angeles road just west of Las Vegas de Santa Clara (a resting place some fifty miles beyond the southward bend of the Virgin River).

Several groups of emigrants tried it—to find themselves wandering in "wild, dreary desolation" between towering mountain walls—perishing of hunger and thirst—waiting for the return of some of their number who had pushed on ahead to beg for aid. One of these men, W. L. Manly, wrote a classic account of the sufferings hinted at in the pictures *right* and *below*.

PULLING THE OXEN DOWN THE PRECIPICE.

LEAVING DEATH VALLEY.—THE MANLY PARTY ON THE MARCH AFTER LEAVING THEIR WAGONS.

Both illustrations on this page are from William Lewis Manly, *Death Valley in '49.* 1894

J. M. Letts, *A Pictorial View of California.* 1853

## AT THE MINES

The northern mining districts attracted the bulk of the first Forty-Niners. Later comers set out, as a rule, for the central and southern districts.

Sacramento City was the focal point for the northern region. It was an exciting sprawl of shops, auction rooms, gambling houses and saloons at the junction of the American and Sacramento Rivers. "The main streets and the levee fronting on the Embarcadero were constantly thronged with the teams of emigrants coming in from the mountains. Their tents were pitched by hundreds in the thickets around town."

One of these tent encampments is seen *above*. The view of Sacramento City *below* shows the Eagle Theatre at the right. For its opening in the fall of 1849, "The Bandit Chief" was offered. The heroine had a strong Cockney accent and the orchestra, in the words of one who was there, consisted of "a fiddle, a very cheezy flageolet played by a gentleman with one eye, a big drum and a triangle——"

William M'Ilvaine, Jr., *Sketches of Scenery and Notes of Personal Adventure in California & Mexico.* 1850.
*Courtesy,* The New-York Historical Society, New York City

The 1849 view of Sacramento City *above* shows a building under construction at the corner of J Street and the levee. Many visitors commented on the pleasant way in which great oaks and sycamores bulked up in backyards; many others commented on the prevailing ague and diarrhoea.

By the time the emigrants arrived at the gold fields, the early birds had moved on from the South Fork of the American River (*below*) to greener fields farther away. Yet the river where the first find had been made was fixed in the popular imagination—and the new arrivals found that rockers and cradles would yield gold in gulches and on bars already deserted by the pick and pan men.

Both illustrations on this page are from J. M. Letts, *A Pictorial View of California.* 1853

J. D. Borthwick, *Three Years in California*. 1857

Above Placerville was Weber Creek, site of the camp *above*, where running water made "panning" easier than at "dry" diggings. A simple bowl or pan, half filled with dirt, was held in the current; large stones were picked out by hand as the stream carried off the earth. At last you had left only a little heavy sand—and gold.

At Mormon Diggings on the North Fork of the American (*below*) cradles were early in use—crude boxes on rockers, with at one end a coarse sieve and at the other small cleats. Four-man teams worked the cradles: one man dug; another carried; a third rocked the machine up and down; the fourth kept water running through. The gold caught against the cleats at the open end. Nuggets above one-half ounce went, not to the team but to the finder.

J. M. Letts, *A Pictorial View of California*. 1853

Nothing discouraged the small parties which struck away from known locations to prospect new territories. They fanned out over all the districts—setting up camp for a night and cooking a simple supper, hopeful that the next day's work with pick and pan would show "a good prospect."

W. R. Ryan, *Personal Adventures in Upper and Lower California in 1848-49.* 1850

W. R. Ryan, *Personal Adventures in Upper and Lower California in 1848-49.* 1850

A. Ferran and J. Baturone, *Album Californiano.*
*Courtesy,* The New-York Historical Society, New York City

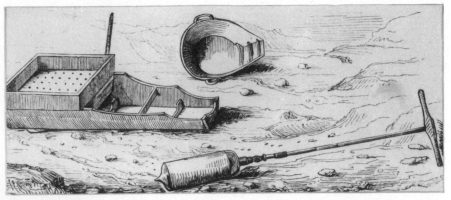

W. R. Ryan, *Personal Adventures in Upper and Lower California in 1848-49*. 1850

One of the Forty-Niners made the sketch at the *left*, which shows a two-man cradle, a pan, and a boring-tool.

Mexicans, long practiced in the mines of Durango and Chihuahua, crowded into California and met with anything but a welcome from the Forty-Niners. By excessive taxes, or by naked force, they were barred from the diggings where Americans were in the majority.

The picture at the *right* shows the Sonoran method of "dry-washing" as practiced by the Mexicans. "Balancing the bowl on one hand, by a quick motion of the other they cause it to revolve, at the same time throwing its contents in the air and catching them as they fall. In this manner, everything is winnowed away except the heavier grains of sand mixed with gold, which are carefully separated by the breath."

John Frost, *History of the State of California*. 1850

The Forty-Niner spent Sunday as shown *left*.

Alonzo Delano, *Pen Knife Sketches; or, Chips of the Old Block*. 1853. *Courtesy*, The Library of Congress, Washington, D. C.

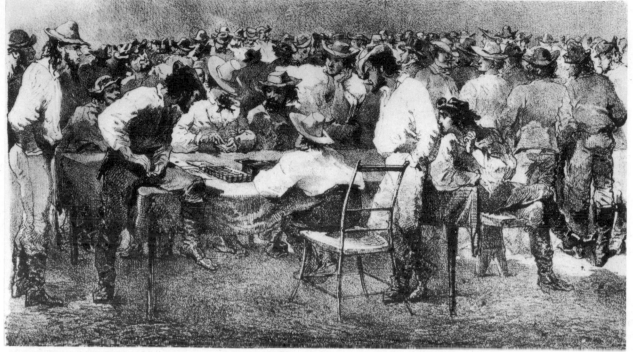

J. D. Borthwick, *Three Years in California.* 1857

When men without immediate responsibility find themselves with pockets full of gold dust, their spare time is not always well spent. Gambling was universal and the monte table (*above*) drew like a magnet. "Our little village boasted of at least a dozen monte tables," wrote one of the Forty-Niners, "all of which were frequented at night."

High spirits, of one kind or another, led to the kind of horseplay pictured *below.*

Alonzo Delano, *Old Block's Sketch-Book; or, Tales of California Life.* 1856

J. D. Borthwick, *Three Years in California.* 1857

The faro tables (*above*) did a thriving business in the mining camps and at Sacramento City
All too little of the precious dust found its way to the banker's assay table (*below*). The cost of
food, clothing and the simplest personal services was so high that much of the mined gold passed
into the hands of carpenters, boarding-house proprietors and land speculators.

Alonzo Delano, *Pen Knife Sketches; or, Chips of the Old Block.* 1853. *Courtesy,* The Library of Congress, Washington, D. C.

# 5

# Southwest the Course

WHEN WIDE-AWAKE citizens of Arkansas realized that many thousands of their fellows were bound and determined to take *some* trail to California, they began to advertise with trumpet blasts the advantages of Fort Smith, on the western edge of Arkansas, as the jumping-off place for California by way of Santa Fe. Philanthropy and the wish to be helpful played some part in this; but a thought of the profits to be made in outfitting the emigrants was not altogether out of their minds. The Arkansas Assembly made representations to Senator Jefferson Davis of Mississippi, and he gave out in January, 1849, an official endorsement of the southwestern route as the one best adapted for use as a national road to the far West.

Many gold-seekers had planned to get the jump on those traveling over the northern overland route by an early departure down the old Santa Fe Trail, starting from Independence, Missouri, or from Westport Landing. But now, as they read glowing accounts in newspapers at Cincinnati, Memphis and other river towns, they were persuaded to abandon the tried and true road by way of the Cimarron, or by Bent's Fort, for one declared to be five hundred miles shorter and abounding in early grass and never-failing water. In addition, the advertisements guaranteed safe arrival at Monterey, California, within sixty days of leaving Fort Smith (*below*).

*U. S. Senate, Executive Document No. 78, 33rd Congress, 2nd Session*

*U. S. Senate, Executive Document No. 78, 33rd Congress, 2nd Session*

But the storekeepers at Van Buren, a town seven miles from Fort Smith around a bend of the Arkansas River, maintained that their goods were cheaper and better than those for sale at the Fort. They cried from the housetops that the road westward from Van Buren was a better road. Be that as it may, white-topped wagons rolled out of both towns—westward through Indian Territory—that spring of 1849.

With loud "gee-haws" and the crack of whips, the emigrants from Van Buren followed, first the Arkansas River, then the north bank of the South Canadian River, to Chouteau's Fort where they crossed to the south bank and met the Fort Smith contingent toiling up on the road from the Choctaw and Shawnee villages.

The first great landmark on this southwestern route was "Rock Mary," *above;* named for a young lady emigrant, Mary Conway, whose charm, beauty and discretion broke hearts all the way to Los Angeles.

A military escort was accompanying the gold-seekers, and hostile Indians kept their distance. For the most part, the road climbed and descended gentle grades beside the placid South Canadian. (*Below.*)

*U. S. Senate, Executive Document No. 438, 29th Congress, 1st Session*

At this stage of the trail, there was little of the stress and excitement that marked the passage westward by the northern overland. The way was smooth, monotonous and easy; the debris of years of travel by Mexicans and Indians was strewn about. The emigrants marvelled at the roughly-hewn axles and square wheels of long-abandoned Spanish *carretas*.

Many small tributaries ran into the Canadian from the southward. Wine Creek (*above*) came in just beyond Dry River, some forty miles west of Antelope Bluffs. At Shady Creek (*below*), was a deserted Comanche camp.

Both illustrations on this page are from *U. S. Senate, Executive Document No. 91, 33rd Congress, 2nd Session*

BORDER OF EL-LLANO ESTACADO

Ackerman Lith 379.

*U. S. Senate, Executive Document No. 54, 32nd Congress, 2nd Session*

Beyond Shady Creek, the bluffs along the border of *El Llano Estacado* came in sight to the south-ward. These were the "Staked Plains" of Texas, which Coronado had seen centuries before; to their fastnesses the fierce Kiowas and Comanches retreated to recruit their strength for new forays. For almost a day, the road of the emigrants passed through a continuous prairie-dog town as shown *below*.

Josiah Gregg, *Commerce of the Prairies.* 1844

The emigrant trains moved along the southwestern route in almost military order. Striving for speed of passage was not encouraged. One of the soldiers who accompanied the emigrants had this to say of the manner in which they made camp on the night of June 15, 1849:

"The first wagon is driven up to its place and halted; the second is then driven up to the left of the first—the tongues being so near to each other that, after the mules are disengaged, they may be made to cross each other. The third wagon is then driven to the right of the first, and so halted that the left fore-wheel of this third wagon will graze or be very near the right hind-wheel of the first wagon; the fourth wagon is then driven to the left of the second—its fore right-wheel grazing the left hind-wheel of the second wagon. Then come in succession, to take their places in like manner, the fifth, sixth, seventh, eighth, etc. . . . that when the enclosure is completed it will be in the form of an ellipse, or circle. The *corral* made, the animals are turned out to graze, and a guard detailed to watch them. Now comes the busy scene of pitching tents, collecting wood, preparing food, etc.

"Some children are playing near the water, and under a large, shady, cottonwood tree on the bank of the stream I see a young lady . . . habited in her riding-dress and with bonnet on, a veil thrown carelessly aside, she is twirling listlessly a switch and giving heed to the conversation of a young emigrant, who is sitting contentedly at her feet."

Whether or not the lady was Mary Conway, we shall never know. Lieutenant Simpson omitted this piece of information. He tells us that there was a dance that night in the camp of the emigrants.

Eight days later, the long line of wagons left the Canadian River and struck for the Pecos River which was crossed at Anton Chico. The view of La Cuesta Valley *below* shows a part of the road between Anton Chico and the junction with the old Santa Fe Trail running down from Bent's Fort.

*U. S. Senate, Executive Document No. 91, 33rd Congress, 2nd Session*

*U. S. Senate, Executive Document No. 438, 29th Congress, 1st Session*

The road into Santa Fe was bordered by cliffs. As the emigrants neared the city, the cliffs broke into a succession of barren hills (*above*), covered in places with a growth of dwarf cedars.

At Santa Fe (*below*, as seen from the east), a population sharpened by years of trade was ready for this unexpected windfall of good fortune. Outfits which had toiled, pleasantly enough, the eight hundred and twenty miles from Fort Smith, were sure to be in need of many things. Santa Fe had them—at a price. To sweeten the bitter draught, there was gambling, entertainment, exotic food, and the *fandango*.

*Courtesy*, Stokes Collection, The New York Public Library, New York City

*U. S. Engineer Bureau, Executive Document No. 41, 30th Congress, 1st Session*

Life was good at Santa Fe. But no emigrant could dream too long in the comfortable shadow of the mission church *above*. There was a hard journey ahead—and thousands of others pressing on behind. The military guard had turned its mules out to graze; besides, it would go no farther than Doña Ana on the Rio Grande. So, as soon as practicable, the emigrants were on the trail again—southward down the Rio Grande—past the mines of Placer Mountain in the Zandias (*below*) with their hint of the golden goal.

*U. S. Senate, Executive Document No. 64, 31st Congress, 1st Session*

*U. S. Senate, Executive Document No. 91, 33rd Congress, 2nd Session*

The trail led through the towns of Albuquerque (*above*); Socorro, where the pack trail turned off toward the headwaters of the River Gila; San Diego. At this last village, Cooke's Wagon Road, the only way by which a wagon train could get through, left the river and dipped southwestward into Mexico. This was the road taken in 1846 by Lt.-Col. P. St.G. Cooke and his Mormons, the while Gen. Kearny and the dragoons had pack-muled down the Gila to "conquer" California.

Emigrants who took the Wagon Road were careful to provide themselves with as much water as they could carry before they turned their backs on the Organ Peaks (*below*).

J. R. Bartlett, *Personal Narrative of Explorations.* 1854

The trail led across grassy country; across the Rio Mimbres whose water was icy-cold and sweet; a hundred and fifty miles to the broken, jagged place of precipitous descents and heart-breaking climbs called Guadaloupe Pass (*above* and *below*).

Both illustrations on this page are from *U. S. Senate, Executive Document No. 108, 34th Congress, 1st Session*

One of the emigrants wrote: "We had to take off our mules and let our wagons down with ropes. After getting to the bottom, we traveled down a canyon for some twelve miles or more [*above*]; crossing a stream that ran through it, some 35 or 40 times in that distance."

At the end of the Guadaloupe Pass, the trail turned northward through San Bernardino Springs (*below*).

Both illustrations on this page are from *U. S. Senate, Executive Document No. 108, 34th Congress, 1st Session*

The valley of Santa Cruz (*above*) was a welcome sight to emigrants who had bulled their way through the Guadaloupe. But its good grass fed few cattle; its beauty was scarred with the ruins of ranches and villages. The Apaches made this lovely valley their special prey. No one could live there in safety.

About a hundred miles up the valley of Santa Cruz lay Tucson (*below*), a town of about five hundred souls, where the wagon trains recruited for the long, dry drive to the Gila, and stocked up with melons, fruit and flour.

Both illustrations on this page are from J. R. Bartlett, *Personal Narrative of Explorations.* 1854

*U. S. House of Representatives, Executive Document No. 91, 33rd Congress, 2nd Session*

At Tucson was an impressive testimony to the one-time energies of Spain; the mission church of San Xavier del Bac *above*.

Few of the emigrants took the time to philosophize over past greatness. For, from Tucson to the villages of the Pima and Maricopa Indians on the Gila River the trail ran seventy-five miles without grass or water. Many of the gold-seekers came to the breaking point on this part of the golden adventure; many of them found graves in the shifting sands. Those who were stronger, or more provident, pushed on and saw at last the dome-shaped lodges of the Pimas through the heat haze of a desert summer.

These broken tribes had been described in the guidebooks as peaceful and honest. The emigrants found them peaceful enough, but no more honest than other Indians, or for that matter than white men. They knew the value of what they had to sell—corn, pumpkins, fodder for the cattle, melons—and even the simplest Indian could tell from the look of men and women who had crossed the desert that their needs would outweigh their inclination to bargain.

On the facing page are three views of the Pimas in their native state as the emigrants saw them.

J. R. Bartlett, *Personal Narrative of Explorations.* 1854

*Above*, to the right, is a typical Pima lodge, built of thatch and mud.

The Pimas and Maricopas were artists with a bow and arrow. At the *right*, they are engaging in their favorite sport—shooting at the spikes of the pitahaya.

*Below* are to be seen some of the fruits of their contact with the emigrants.

J. R. Bartlett, *Personal Narrative of Explorations.* 1854

U. S. Senate, *Executive Document No. 108, 34th Congress, 1st Session*

# THE PACK TRAIL

Cooke's Wagon Road was a waste of time, said the more impatient emigrants. Hadn't General Kearny headed straight west from the Rio Grande to the Pima villages? True, he couldn't take wagons: but if wagons were going to prevent early arrival in the golden country . . . ! So, without thought of what might lie beyond the Pima towns, many of the gold-seekers packed supplies on their mules, abandoned their wagons and struck westward from the valley of the Rio Grande at the place shown *above*, some two hundred miles south of Santa Fe.

After five or six days of mountain trails, they reached the arid valley of the Gila River (*below*).

Both illustrations on this page are from W. H. Emory, *Notes of a Military Reconnoissance, from Fort Leavenworth to San Diego.* 1848

W. H. Emory, *Notes of a Military Reconnoissance, from Fort Leavenworth to San Diego.* 1848

They crossed and re-crossed the Gila, making slow way along an incredibly rough road. They made camp near giant cacti, under the shadow of fantastically eroded cliffs (*above*).

To the southward lay waste valleys through which flowed tributaries of the Gila. The view *below* looks up the valley of the Aravaypa toward its junction with the San Pedro.

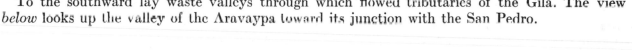

*U. S. House of Representatives, Executive Document No. 91, 33rd Congress, 2nd Session*

*U. S. Senate, Executive Document No. 108, 34th Congress, 1st Session*

Soon the Pima villages were known to be near. Friendly tribesmen came out to meet the pack trains, as the exhausted emigrants stumbled along. Shirts and blankets were the best trade goods with which to bargain for fresh food.

And now the double tide of emigrants, those who had packed down the Gila from its upper reaches and those who had come up from Tucson, joined and moved down the valley of the Gila River in intense heat and with a sober dread of what was to come.

Behind the mountains in the view of the Gila Valley *below* lay the short-cut known as the "Jornada de las Estrellas" which was supposed to save time and only added to the sufferings of those who tried it.

*U. S. House of Representatives, Executive Document No. 91, 33rd Congress, 2nd Session*

*U. S. House of Representatives, Executive Document No. 91, 33rd Congress, 2nd Session*

The heat and dry air were shrinking the wooden parts of the wagons. Tires ran off the wheels; bodies began to fall to pieces. Grass could be got for the worn-out animals only by swimming them to the bars and islands in the river's thread. On this part of the route, between the bend of the Gila (*above*) or Big Horn Mountain (*below*) and the edge of the desert—sixteen days' travel away—tragedies began to multiply. Many of the emigrants were pushing dumbly along on foot. Mules were dead; food was gone; up ahead was the junction of the Gila and the Colorado—and the desert!

J. R. Bartlett, *Personal Narrative of Explorations.* 1854

Desperate measures were tried. Some parties went down the Gila on rafts hastily built of drift-wood, running into bars, upsetting, losing all their goods.

At the crossing of the Colorado River, about eight miles southwest of its junction with the Gila (*below*), anything which would float was pressed into service—wagon beds caulked so as to be water-tight, canoes, rafts. Many drowned as the frail craft overturned. And always, the dreaded and warlike Yuma Indians hovered around the crossing—raiding down from the rocky cliffs on the exhausted wagon trains and pack trains—looting stock and food—sometimes killing. As much heavy equipment was abandoned as could be spared. The Gila Valley from the Pima villages to Colorado crossing was as much an enormous junk shop as was Ragtown on the Carson.

Those who still had animals waited a few days at the crossing, pulling grass, curing and twisting it into hay, gathering mesquite leaves and beans, all in preparation for the ninety miles of desert that lay between Yuma country and Vallecito, the first of the California settlements. Water was stored in gourds purchased from the Pimas.

If the Sierra were the "Elephant" on the northern overland, the "Elephant" of the Southwest was this fearful desert of scorching, salt sand and shifting hills. Facing it with them were the few gold-seekers who had struck due west at Albuquerque and traveled what they thought was a shorter road, through the old Indian town of Zuni.

J. R. Bartlett, *Personal Narrative of Explorations.* 1854

# WESTWARD BY ZUNI

*U. S. Senate, Executive Document No. 91, 33rd Congress, 2nd Session.*

"At Camp Number 2, west of Zuni [*above*] were remains of a camp, probably one of those made by Lt. Thom who escorted Mr. Collier to California in 1849," observed Lieutenant Sitgreaves two years later.

*U. S. Senate, Executive Document No. 64, 31st Congress, 1st Session*

They would have gazed up at the peak of San Francisco Mountain (*right*).

This party would have passed Inscription Rock (*left*), bearing names of those who had passed that way as early as 1605.

*U. S. Senate, Executive Document No. 91, 33rd Congress, 2nd Session*

Over the kind of country shown *above*, they would have journeyed to the valley of Bill Williams Fork. The view *below* was made near the beaver dams beyond the mouth of Big Sandy Creek.

Both illustrations on this page are from *U. S. Senate, Executive Document No. 91, 33rd Congress, 2nd Session*

Bill Williams Fork emptied into the great Colorado (*above*). Then the trail turned southward through the country of the Mohave Indians and came eventually to Yuma, where the Gila joined the Colorado (*below*).

When Collier's party reached the banks of the Gila, some few miles above the junction, they met a tattered crowd of gold hunters who had made their way by an incredible route across Texas and Mexico. One of this group was John W. Audubon, but his story must wait for a later chapter.

Both illustrations on this page are from *U. S. Senate, Executive Document No. 59, 32nd Congress, 2nd Session*

# THE DESERT

"... a number of men, lank and brown 'as is the ribbed sea-sand' —men with long hair and beards, and faces from which the rigid expression of suffering was scarcely relaxed. These were the first of the overland emigrants by the Gila route, who had reached San Diego a few days before. Their clothes were in tatters, their boots in many cases replaced by moccasins and except for their rifles and some small packages rolled in deerskin, they had nothing left of the abundant stores with which they left home."

In these words, the New York *Tribune's* correspondent, Mr. Bayard Taylor, described those whom the desert had marked—those who had survived. He was himself fresh from what he had considered the rigors of the route across the Isthmus of Panama: these scarecrow men made him feel that the overcrowding and foul food on the steamship *Panama* had been minor indeed.

*Gleason's Pictorial*, Mar. 27, 1852

*Below* is seen the point near Pilot Knob in the valley of the Colorado, where the emigrants first ventured out onto the deep sands—on mule-back, on foot, or walking beside their wagons.

*U. S. Senate, Executive Document No. 91, 33rd Congress, 2nd Session*

The wells in the desert (*above,* the well at Alamo Mocho) were soon spoiled as men and animals greedily drained what water was in them.

"Broken wagons, dead shriveled-up cattle, horses and mules as well, lay baking in the sun around the dried-up wells."

The stench from the carcasses hung on the air. The wind stirred the sand across the dried clay of the wells with a low, rustling sound, infinitely mournful.

The temperature stood at 110°. There was no shade. The mesquite bushes drooped in the sun.

Both illustrations on this page are from *U. S. Senate, Executive Document No. 91, 33rd Congress, 2nd Session*

*U. S. Senate, Executive Document No. 91, 33rd Congress, 2nd Session*

Sometimes a mirage tantalized the travelers as they plodded slowly through the sand. The appearance of tall, minareted cities on the horizon *above* was only the heat-distorted image of distant mountains.

The interminable trail wound on. The bones of men and animals reminded the emigrants of what they would have preferred to forget *(below)*: But the wall of the *cordillera* was in sight, and almost miraculously a stream had appeared in the desert which the emigrants called Salvation River or New River.

*U. S. Senate, Executive Document No. 108, 34th Congress, 1st Session*

*U. S. Senate, Executive Document No. 108, 34th Congress, 1st Session*

At Carrizo Creek (*above*) the desert contracted within barren ranges of hills. Soon strange outcroppings of rock began to rise from the sand (*below*).

*U. S. Senate, Executive Document No. 91, 33rd Congress, 2nd Session*

By the pass *above*, the emigrants crossed from Vallecito to San Felipe. Here at last, the way-worn men and women, ragged, dusty, leading their jaded animals, had reached green country again. The water at Vallecito tasted of sulphur, but it was water. At San Felipe, there was plenty of good water, and grass; and Warner's Pass (*below*) was in sight from San Felipe—the last barrier!

Both illustrations on this page are from *U. S. Senate, Executive Document No. 91, 33rd Congress, 2nd Session*

The desert, the Indians, the mountains, thirst, hunger, disillusion—none of these had downed the spirits of those hardy souls who came pouring into San Diego (*right*). Many were on foot, and ready to tell anyone who would listen what fine outfits they had lost— what splendid animals the Yumas had stolen from them at the crossing of the Colorado.

W. H. Emory, *Notes of a Military Reconnoissance, from Fort Leavenworth to San Diego.* 1848

Two survivors of the "Knickerbocker Company" bought a wagon at San Diego Mission (*below*) and filled it with vegetables. They had heard that fresh food was selling high in the gold districts, and the desert had not blunted their sense of business.

*U. S. Senate, Executive Document No. 91, 33rd Congress, 2nd Session*

# NORTH TO THE MINES

Bayard Taylor, *Eldorado, or Adventures in the Path of Empire.* 1850

Monterey (*above*) marked the dividing line between the agricultural country to the south, whose languor was stirred only by land speculation, and the wild hurly-burly of the gold country. To go north as quickly as possible was the aim of every emigrant—to go where the gold was. The horse markets (*below*) were doing a land-office business. There was talk of new strikes in the San Joaquin Valley.

Frank Marryat, *Mountains and Molehills.* 1855. *Courtesy,* The New-York Historical Society, New York City

Overcrowding, jealousy of others' success, the bickering of bored men in a strictly masculine society, all these were creating in the camps a spirit very different from the happy-go-lucky spirit which had prevailed through the earlier half of 1849. Tempers were hair-trigger.

Alonzo Delano, *Old Block's Sketch-Book; or, Tales of California Life.* 1856

The regions about the American, the Cosumnes and the Mokelumne Rivers were still the scenes of greatest activity. As Bayard Taylor took the trail over steep spurs to the Lower Bar diggings on the Mokelumne (*below*), he noted that the companies of miners had built dams in order to divert the water and lay the river bed bare. Every part of the gulch had been explored by the picks of the gold-seekers.

Bayard Taylor, *Eldorado, or Adventures in the Path of Empire.* 1850

Questions of law were settled by locally-elected *alcaldes*. Penalties for stealing were especially severe because of the near impossibility of replacing the simplest articles. At open-air courts like the one shown *left*, shaving the head, the loss of an ear, or a hundred lashes might be the price of thieving.

Frank Marryat, *Mountains and Molehills*. 1855. *Courtesy*, The New-York Historical Society, New York City

The road to the Volcano diggings (*below*) lay up the valley of the Mokelumne and over a divide. Polo, the wily chief of the local Indians, had declared war on the miners, and the trail through the thick woods was far from safe in the autumn of 1849. Polo's braves had discovered these placers first; the whites had come later and driven them away.

Bayard Taylor, *Eldorado, or Adventures in the Path of Empire*. 1850

In some localities, there were tawny, half-Indian beauties (*right*) who were the belles of the *fandango* before an increasing number of female Americans pre-empted that social eminence.

J. Ross Browne, *Crusoe's Island.* 1864

But with women or without them, the miners celebrated holidays with brandy, champagne and song. A stag "dance" like the one pictured *below* might go on for days and end only when the revelers "lay about in heaps on the floor, howling, barking and roaring."

J. D. Borthwick, *Three Years in California.* 1857

# SAN FRANCISCO

W. R. Ryan, *Personal Adventures in Upper and Lower California in 1848-49*. 1850

The gold-seekers who took ship from San Diego or Los Angeles at the end of the southwestern trail found San Francisco (*above*, in 1849) a feverish tent-town, with on every side "buildings of all kinds, begun or half-finished, and the greater part of them mere canvas sheds open in front and covered with signs in all languages." Portsmouth Square (*below*) boasted the "El Dorado" gambling house and the "Parker House" hotel, a frame structure whose second floor was occupied entirely by gamblers.

Bayard Taylor, *Eldorado, or Adventures in the Path of Empire*. 1850

For more than a mile around the curve of the Bay, hundreds of tents and buildings were scattered over the heights and along the shore. Abandoned ships served as warehouses and hotels—great quantities of goods were piled up in the open for want of places to store them. The price of goods and the price of skilled labor had skyrocketed out of sight. It was cheaper to buy a new shirt and throw the dirty one away than to have it washed and ironed. Fastidious folk who had brought fine linen with them and prized it, sent their wash by clipper ship to Canton or Honolulu for laundering.

San Francisco was a bewildering place in the fall of 1849.

All kinds of people flitted restlessly through the streets—carefully dressed gamblers, miners down for a spending spree, Kanakas, Chinese, Chileans, Frenchmen, Peruvians, Germans, the men who had crossed the plains and the mountains, the men who had survived the merciless sun of the Gila and the Colorado desert.

Through gaps in the hills, the wind kept the sand whipping up from the unpaved streets. But late in the season, unusually heavy rains set in and reduced the streets to the condition shown *below*.

Frank Marryat, *Mountains and Molehills.* 1855. *Courtesy,* The New-York Historical Society, New York City

Frank Marryat, *Mountains and Molehills.* 1855. *Courtesy,* The New-York Historical Society, New York City

The visitor hadn't far to go for a game of chance. Dozens of gambling houses stood around Portsmouth Square—Denison's Exchange, the El Dorado, the St. Charles, the Bella Union. At the end of the gambling room was always a bar *(above)*, "supplied with all kinds of bad liquor." The El Dorado featured a muscular lady violinist—across the square at the Verandah, there was a "one-man band." Even in a humble place like the ship's cabin made into a shore restaurant as shown *below*, breakfast cost one dollar.

W. R. Ryan, *Personal Adventures in Upper and Lower California in 1848-49.* 1850

# Isthmus and Mexico

COMFORTABLE MEN in the seaboard states, men of assured financial position, shrewd men of affairs, these were not the least eager among the gold-rushers of 1849. They may have thought that success in the search for gold would demonstrate their superiority over common folk. Possibly, the adventurous nature of the enterprise challenged that bit of the national restlessness deep in their souls. Whatever the reason, these solid men joined the race for fortune with as much, and more, enthusiasm, than the "Pikes," as poor emigrants from Missouri and Arkansas were called.

No wagons or ox teams for the solid men! They were used to long voyages by sea, rather than by land; and yet they were not taken in by the flamboyant promises on the posters which advertised everywhere the all-water route around Cape Horn. That was the safest route, by all odds, but the solid men wanted a way to the golden country which would be short, speedy and comfortable. Any intelligent man had only to look at a map to know which was the only perfect route. Damme, sir, look there! Only seventy-five miles across the Isthmus of Panama, from the port of Chagres on the Atlantic side to Panama City on the Pacific Ocean itself! Only seventy-five miles of inconvenience, and open at all seasons of the year, mind you!

The new mail-steamer service stood ready to take most of the difficulty out of the trip. Through tickets were on sale: New York to Chagres by steamer—the Isthmus—and then a connecting Pacific Mail steamer at Panama City, waiting to whisk you directly up the coast to San Francisco. Meanwhile, not a day went by but sailing ships left New York and New Orleans for Chagres. A rapid passage to the Isthmus might make it worth a gold-seeker's while to take his chances on the connection at Panama City. A fortunate man might save as much as two weeks' time!

Others among the solid men were attracted by the ease and safety of the routes to California across Mexico. Some of them had served in the recent war with that tumultuous republic. They flattered themselves that its mountain trails were an open book to them. Without pausing to think that the Mexicans might not welcome another visit from North Americans, however pacific, they formed the inevitable "companies for mutual aid and protection," shipped their heavy goods around Cape Horn, and in the warm atmosphere of New York and Boston drawing-rooms planned to march westward from Vera Cruz to Mexico City and thence to some port on the western coast where a ship might be had for San Francisco.

A few solid men hoped to steal a march on everyone else by heading across Texas and northern Mexico, starting either from the mouth of the Rio Grande, or from Corpus Christi, a little farther up the coast of the Gulf of Mexico. They would take a ship at Mazatlan, or any other convenient port on the Pacific Ocean side.

## THE ISTHMUS

With sublime faith in the power of ready cash to ward off dysentery, yellow fever and cholera, to make water spring up in desert places, and to buy passage aboard ships already awash with expectant millionaires, the solid men pored over their maps and convinced themselves that their very own road was the safest, quickest and most genteel.

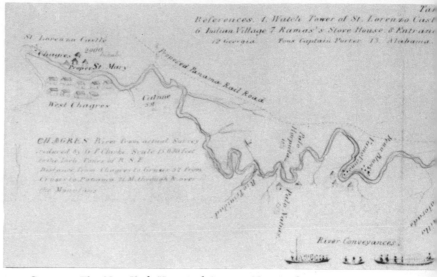

*Courtesy*, The New-York Historical Society, New York City

The 1850 map of the route across the Isthmus of Panama shown *above*, gives a graphic presentation of the modes of travel, and the distances from point to point.

The Panama route attracted another sort of adventurer, in addition to its proportion of the solid men—gentry more used to relying on their wits than on their bank accounts—men like the "long, loosely-jointed men" Bayard Taylor saw come aboard his ship at New Orleans.

"Their faces were lengthened and deeply sallow, overhung by straggling locks of straight, black hair, and wore an expression of settled melancholy. The corners of their mouths curved downwards, the upper lip drawn slightly over the under one, giving to the lower part of the face that cast of destructiveness peculiar to the Indian. These men chewed tobacco at a ruinous rate and spent their time either in dozing at full length on the deck or going into the fore-cabin for 'drinks.' Each one of them carried enough arms for a whole company, and breathed defiance to all foreigners."

On the way from New York to Chagres, the steamers stopped at Kingston on the island of Jamaica to fill their coal bunkers. As seen at the *right*, this could be a long operation, for the porters were native women who carried the baskets of coal on their heads.

*Courtesy*, Stokes Collection, The New York Public Library, New York City

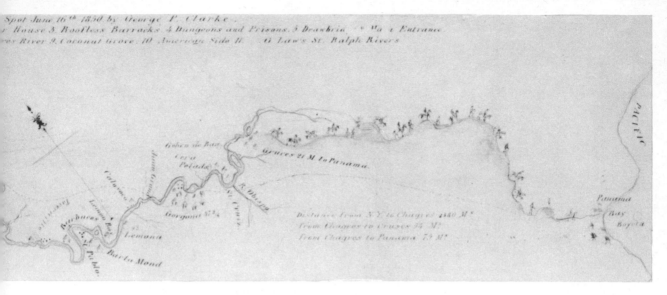

The map left to the gold-seeker's imagination, however, the climate of the Isthmus, the rain, the swamps, the fevers, the scorpions and snakes of New Granada.

*Courtesy,* The New-York Historical Society, New York City

Chagres is shown *above,* as it looked to the gold-seekers. The castle of San Lorenzo stands on the bluff at the left; the entrance to the Chagres River is at the extreme right.

"The old castle crowns the point, occupying a position somewhat similar to the Morro at Havana . . . Morgan and his buccaneers scaled its walls and took it after a fight in which all but thirty-three out of three hundred and fourteen defenders were slain . . ."

So soon as a vessel dropped anchor, native canoes or dug-outs were on hand to offer passage up the river and through the jungles to Gorgona or Cruces where the pack roads began. Bargains were struck; money changed hands; faithful promises were made.

But the eager passengers had not counted on the whims and languor of tropic peoples. When baggage had been unloaded and piled on the shore, the boatmen were no longer in the mood to travel. They sat in the mud beside their beached canoes. They smoked cigars in the doorways of their thatched huts. They loafed and invited their souls.

At the thought that other men might be beating them to the gold, the frustrated *Americanos* raged up and down the beach. The one hotel was filled. Food was to be had only in the native huts. Minutes, hours were going by!

Then began the competitive bidding for passage. Five dollars—eight dollars—fifteen dollars apiece for passage to the head of the river—*pronto!* The natives began to take the cigars out of their mouths and consider.

J. M. Letts, *A Pictorial View of California.* 1853

When the rate of pay had been arranged to their satisfaction, the boatmen hefted their broad paddles, strolled down to the riverside, and with a few practiced strokes sent the canoe up the Chagres, away from the noise and confusion of the town to the beauty and seclusion of the river. Native canoes are seen at the mouth of the Chagres River in the view *above.*

A Panama "bongo," or sailing-canoe, is shown at the *left.*

F. N. Otis, *Illustrated History of the Panama Railroad.* 1861

Frank Marryat, *Mountains and Molehills*. 1855. Courtesy, The New-York Historical Society, New York City

*Above,* a scene on the early reaches of the Chagres River.

"There is nothing in the world comparable to these forests . . . The river, broad, and with a swift current of the sweetest water I ever drank, winds between walls of foliage that rise from its very surface . . . From the rank jungle of cane and gigantic lilies, and the thickets of strange shrubs that line the water, rise the trunks of the mango, the ceiba, the cocoa, the sycamore and the superb palm."

"Blossoms of crimson, purple and yellow, of a form and magnitude unknown in the North, are mingled with the leaves, and flocks of paroquets and brilliant butterflies circle through the air like blossoms blown away. Sometimes a spike of scarlet flowers is thrust forth like the tongue of a serpent from the heart of some convolution of unfolding leaves, and often the creepers and parasites drop trails and streamers of fragrance from boughs that shoot halfway across the river."

The first stop after Chagres was Gatun—a village of bamboo huts on the right bank of the river. At Gatun, the boatmen arranged for their employers to spend the afternoon and the first hours of the night in some of the native houses. A notched pole served as a ladder from the common room downstairs to the sleeping loft under the thatch. Over the cane floor were spread musty and ancient hides, the abiding place of innumerable fleas.

Some of the gold-seekers avoided the native houses and pitched their tents on the river bank, as seen *above*. They broke out the rice and dried pork which they had bought at the town of Chagres, split a little firewood and cooked supper.

For the first time, many of the Americans became acquainted with the tropical custom of the *siesta*. In the view *below*, a lady of New Granada is seen in repose. The hammock was swung purposely low to furnish the dogs and other domestic animals a convenient solid point for scratching their backs.

Both illustrations on this page are from J. M. Letts, *A Pictorial View of California*. 1853

J. M. Letts, *A Pictorial View of California.* 1853

The best hours for travel on the Chagres River were the hours between midnight and sunrise. Beset by sudden squalls of rain, so violent that "it seemed as if the sky had caved in," the adventurers wrapped themselves in rubber *ponchos* and envied the singing boatmen who did not seem at all bothered by the wet.

On the second night after leaving the town of Chagres, the character of the river changed; there was less of the jungle along the banks; cultivated fields began to be seen. And the river, swelled by the rains, developed rapids (*above*) which were stemmed with great difficulty.

Even in the short time that the Isthmus had been traversed by our countrymen, the natives had become exceedingly wary and unfriendly. Too many blustering blow-hards had clapped pistols to their heads and sworn strange oaths at them; had eaten their food without paying for it; and had haggled over the price at the end of a tough pull up the river to Gorgona or Cruces.

But if the native boatmen were treated well, they used their influence with friends in the villages and *haciendas* along the way to provide some variation in the diet of dried pork and coffee. Chicken, eggs, rice boiled in cocoa milk and baked plantains made up a typical Panamanian dinner.

The usual point of departure from the river was at the town of Cruces. A mule path led from there over the lower spurs of the broken mountain chain directly to Panama City. But ominous rumors drifted back from boat to boat: *"Cruces . . . mucha colera!"* The same dread disease which was playing so much havoc on the Missouri River and the Platte now levied its toll on the solid men and their "comfortable" route to the gold regions.

The boatmen nosed their canoes into the bank at the town of Gorgona and refused to go any farther. They had not contracted to run the risk of a particularly noisome death. The road over the mountains from Gorgona to Panama City was long and hard, but it was reported to be passable. Horses and mules for transport were very scarce, and the cost of their hire correspondingly high. Many of the gold-seekers packed bare necessities on their backs and set off on foot.

"The path at the outset was bad enough," wrote one of them, "but as the wood grew deeper and darker and the tough clay soil held the rains which had fallen, it became finally a narrow gulley, filled with mud nearly to our horses' bellies. Descending the steep sides of the hills, they would step or slide down almost precipitous passes . . .

"The only sounds in that leafy wilderness were the chattering of monkeys as they cracked the palm-nuts, and the scream of parrots . . . In the deep ravines, spent mules lay dead, and high above them on the large boughs the bald vultures waited silently for us to pass.

Frank Marryat, *Mountains and Molehills*. 1855. *Courtesy*, The New-York Historical Society, New York City

At about half-way to Panama City, the trail climbed out on a level tableland covered with palm trees. Beyond it rose a higher ridge. In the swamps and thickets on the descent from this ridge, many a man had the experience shown *right*.

Alonzo Delano, *Old Block's Sketch-Book; or, Tales of California Life.* 1856

These swamps and brakes continued all the way to a point where the trace of an ancient paved road was picked up. It was said that this road led into Panama, but as only vestiges of it were left, and as ridge succeeded rolling ridge without seeming change, the first spurt of hope soon subsided. The gold-seekers pushed on doggedly. If a man felt the cholera coming on him, he turned away from the road and lay down in the thickets to die.

When the Indian guide paused to wash his face and put on his trousers, it meant that the end of the journey was near.

James Delavan, *Notes on California and the Placers.* 1850. *Courtesy,* The New-York Historical Society, New York City

T. T. Johnson, *Sights in The Gold Region.* 1850. *Courtesy,* The Bancroft Library, University of California, Berkeley, Calif.

Even after the tropic rains along the river, the exposure, the bad food, the back-breaking days on the mountain trails, further grief waited for the travelers at Panama City. The city is shown *above,* as it looked in 1849 to J. Pendergast, Esquire, described in one of the earliest published books on the gold rush as "an amateur California artist of the highest attainments."

The solid men, led on to believe that their comfortable route to El Dorado would progress with all the smoothness and efficiency of an urban trip "downtown," found the crumbling Spanish city fairly humming with indignant Americans. Amid the ruined churches and palaces, grass-grown plazas and dry fountains, stranded gold-seekers milled restlessly about and cursed the fine promises of the Pacific Mail Steamship Company. One of the vessels scheduled to "make connection" at Panama City was being repaired. Another steamer, booked solid for San Francisco, had taken aboard seventy-two Peruvian adventurers at Callao. On arrival at Panama City, the captain had little consolation to offer disappointed ticket-holders. The Peruvians refused to vacate; the American consul shrugged his shoulders. In order to give adequate expression to their wrath, those who were left behind founded a newspaper, the "Panama Star."

Meanwhile, on the eastern side of the Isthmus, the steamers unloaded more and more human freight at Chagres. The river was choked with overloaded canoes; on the mountain roads, Chagres fever, dysentery and cholera struck harder and harder.

On top of all this striving and suffering came the delay at Panama City that might consume as much as a month of precious time. It was an item for which few of the solid men had budgeted.

With each dollar that had to be spent for food and lodging, the means of buying or bribing oneself aboard a steamer diminished.

Many disappointed gold-seekers resigned themselves to a seventy or eighty day voyage on a windjammer. There was no lack of sailing craft to take them to California. Some few deluded ones tried to persuade native boatmen to undertake the trip in canoes!

Those who persisted in waiting for the steamer might amuse themselves in the highways and byways of the old Spanish city. The town hall is shown *right;* the Cathedral of Panama, *below.*

F. N. Otis, *Illustrated History of the Panama Railroad.* 1861

J. M. Letts, *A Pictorial View of California.* 1853

Life aboard a steamship on the Panama-San Francisco run in 1849 was a fascinating revelation of selfishness and blackguardism. Crowded fore and aft, deck and cabin, a solid man lucky enough to win passage soon shed any refined inhibitions of conduct. He fought his way to a hammock, if he wanted to sleep; he fought his way to the table, if he wanted to eat.

"The breakfast hour was nine . . . At the first tinkle of the bell, all hands started as if a shot had exploded among them; conversation was broken off in the middle of a word; the deck was instantly cleared, and the passengers, tumbling pell-mell down the cabin-stairs, found every seat taken by others who had been sitting in them for half an hour. The bell, however, had had an equally convulsive effect on these sitters. There was a confused grabbing motion for a few seconds, and lo! the plates were cleared. A chicken parted in twain, as if by magic, each half leaping into an opposite plate."

And so it went, as the ship headed across the Gulf of Tehuantepec, the sea tranquil, the sunsets a glory of crimson and purple. Although the temperature rarely rose above ninety degrees, the humidity made the days intolerable. A great apathy possessed the voyagers.

After a week at sea, the Mexican mountains were sighted in the distance. Next day, the ship made the harbor of Acapulco (*below*), where a small boat came out with news that no one would be allowed ashore for fear of cholera. Unhappy Americans were waiting at Acapulco, hoping that some ship might take them aboard after their long journey across Mexico from Vera Cruz. But there was no room for them.

J. M. Letts, *A Pictorial View of California.* 1853

More gold-seekers were waiting at Manzanillo (*right*); and at Mazatlan (*below*). To this latter port, most of the voyagers across Mexico had directed their steps, for it was the point nearest California on the Mexican Pacific coast from which passage might be had.

J. R. Bartlett, *Personal Narrative of Explorations.* 1854

After clearing Mazatlan, the ship ran around Cape San Lucas, the rugged point of Lower California, and then turned northward. The air grew cooler, as the northwest trade winds began to be felt. When the harbor of San Diego was in sight, there was no longer any depression aboard ship. For the bay of San Francisco would soon be reached—the Golden Gate!

Bayard Taylor, *Eldorado, or Adventures in the Path of Empire.* 1850

# A MEXICAN JOURNEY

Each one of the little groups waiting at Acapulco or San Blas or Mazatlan had its story of privation and hardship—its tale of the harsh journey over the mountains of Mexico from Tampico or Vera Cruz.

One of these Mexican stories may serve for all—the story of Colonel Webb's company from New York. John W. Audubon, son of the great naturalist, went with the Webb party. His journal and the drawings he made on the way are a unique record of a little-known gold rush episode.

Henry Webb was a Colonel by virtue of his command of a regiment of volunteers in the war with Mexico. He formed his company of gold-seekers, financed it privately, and chose a Mexican route because he thought it would permit an early start. Audubon took care of the preliminary organization, and under his command the company left New York early in February, 1849. They traveled by railroad, stagecoach and river boat as far as Cairo, Illinois, where the Colonel joined them and assumed command. At New Orleans they tarried a while, but soon they were able to get passage for Brazos Santiago, the desolate sand-spit at the mouth of the Rio Grande where part of Scott's army had concentrated for the attack on Vera Cruz in 1847.

By March 10, 1849, the Webb company had reached Rio Grande City. On the way there, they had passed Brownsville, Texas (*below*). A letter written home by an already disheartened adventurer described Brownsville as "full of blacklegs and gamblers—not a school or a church in the place."

*U. S. Senate, Executive Document No. 108, 34th Congress, 1st Session*

J. W. Audubon, *Illustrated Notes of an Expedition Through Mexico and California.* 1852

Across the river from Rio Grande City, the Webb company set up a camp (*above*) and began to make final preparations for the hard part of the journey. But disasters multiplied on them. A great part of their cash was stolen, and so the sinews of the journey were untwisted. Then cholera struck down ten of the men. More deserted and started back to New York—chief among them Colonel Webb, who had had enough.

Audubon, himself stricken lightly with cholera, reorganized the men who stuck by the project, saw that the sick were nursed back to health, and on April 28 set off for Chihuahua by the main road through Saltillo. He hoped to strike the junction of the Gila and the Colorado rivers by traversing the mountains of northern Mexico, and to follow thereafter the emigrant road from Yuma across the California desert (see pages 93-98). He had been informed that the pine forests of the mountain country were full of game, and that the climate was a healthy one.

"We approached Saltillo over a broad plain," said Audubon, "dotted with ranches for some miles before we reached the town . . . High mountains bounded our view on all sides."

The view *above* shows the valley leading to Saltillo, as sketched by Captain Whiting of the Seventh Infantry when he happened along that way on government business in 1847.

J. W. Audubon, *Illustrated Notes of an Expedition Through Mexico and California.* 1852

With a confident face and a mind disquieted, Audubon led his men across barren mountain country to the mining town of Parral. He was none too certain that the road by way of Chihuahua was the proper one. There was much talk of Apache raids that would have to be fought off. And at Parral three of the men fell sick. Cholera claimed one of them.

On the advice of some Americans whom he found living in the town, he decided to strike farther to the west and approach the Gila junction by way of the mountains of Sonora.

At first he found the route an interesting one. There were new specimens of plant and animal life which were bound to please an Audubon. But the long days of marching went by without any seeming progress. Up one ridge and down another; and the mules began to fail!

On the Fourth of July, 1849, the party encamped at the spot shown *above*, near the Paso Chapadaro.

Then followed two weeks of journeying through the mountains by trails so narrow and steep that horses and mules had to be led along them. And there were violent storms, which moved one of the party to utter a masterpiece of understatement. "The thunder and lightning are very well done in this country," said he.

On July 18, Audubon noted in his journal: "Our road today was by far the most tedious we have had, being up hill nearly all the time . . . We arrived at the highest top near Jesus Maria —miles of mountain tops and peaks of rock and woods are far below us. Through a gap we looked at clouds blending with the mists below them, until the scene was like an ocean view.

"Four hours and a half of most precipitous descent brought us to a luxuriant growth of pine and spruce and through one of the wildest and most picturesque gorges I have ever seen . . ."

This was the canyon leading down to the little town of Jesus Maria. Audubon's view of the gorge is shown at the *right*.

J. W. Audubon, *Illustrated Notes of an Expedition Through Mexico and California.* 1852

J. W. Audubon, *Illustrated Notes of an Expedition Through Mexico and California.* 1852

At the *left* is Audubon's picture of what he called "the extraordinary little town of Jesus Maria."

It was a tiny village where gold and silver were mined; the ore was crushed in an *arrastre* powered by two mountain torrents which joined together just beyond the place. Audubon found the Mexican miners "half-civilized"; a thing not too remarkable in view of the ten days' travel over rocky roads which intervened between Jesus Maria and the nearest town.

The rest of the adventure is easily told. The town of Altar was reached on September 9. Audubon's party then crossed a "desert-like plain or prairie for many miles." After four days of the desert, they came to a tumble-down rancho where a cow was purchased and her flesh distributed among the men. Thereafter, for the twenty leagues which lay between that place and the Pima villages, there was only bread—and water when they could find it. Lizards, rattlesnakes and toads were the sum of animal life encountered. The pack animals suffered for want of grass. It was only after two weeks of wandering that "we came unexpectedly upon the wagon trail of the Gila route and an exclamation of joy came from almost every one." On page 93 we have already seen the condition in which Audubon's men reached the Gila.

From the Pima villages to San Diego, Audubon and his men shared in the misfortunes that were common to all emigrants by the Gila route.

# IN CALIFORNIA

Ships—sail and steam—from the Isthmus of Panama, from Mazatlan and San Diego, from Valparaiso and Callao, from Papeete in the far-off Society Islands, from Sydney and Honolulu, Canton and Hong Kong, threaded their way through the hundreds of vessels already moored in San Francisco harbor and let go their anchors as close to the wharves as they could get. Little bumboats swarmed out to the ships and ferried the hordes of gold-seekers ashore at a dollar a head.

The passengers, many of them dubious characters indeed, came to a city already self-conscious, confident; still booming and building. A German emigrant who had arrived in San Francisco in the fall of 1849 returned for a visit in January, 1850. He was dumb-struck at the material progress which had been made.

"I had left tents, and low huts and shanties, only two months before; and there were now regular streets of high wooden, and even here and there brick, buildings. But if the habitations had improved, the streets had become proportionally worse . . . they seemed to be only a liquid and moving mass of soft, chocolate-colored mud. In going from one house to another you had to wade through it, and crossing a street seemed a matter of life and death. Many places became really impassable, and in Clay and Montgomery Streets, mules were several times drowned in the middle of the road."

Our visiting German had a sharp eye. He noted that "San Francisco seemed also to be crowded with laborers who had sought the shelter of the town, preferring a sure gain to the uncertain toil of gold-digging."

The view of San Francisco *below* was drawn early in the winter of 1849.

Bayard Taylor, *Eldorado, or Adventures in the Path of Empire.* 1850

On December 16, 1849, Mr. Daniel Knower stayed at the American Hotel, San Francisco (*right*). He felt that he had been robbed when he paid fourteen dollars a day for room and board. But all other costs were in proportion. Money could be borrowed at fourteen percent per month. The price of lumber ranged between three and four hundred dollars a thousand feet. Board shacks in favorable locations rented at prices higher than mansions of stone and brick in New York or Boston. Fortunes had been built by dizzy speculation in this lath and paper grandeur; they were to be swept away by fires which devastated San Francisco through 1850 and 1851.

Sometimes the mails from the east were held up as much as three months. Then the crowds would gather in ugly mood outside the San Francisco Post Office (*below*) and curse Postmaster Moore.

AMERICAN HOTEL.

CORNER OF BROADWAY AND STOCKTON STREET.

W. R. LOUNT......PROPRIETOR.

Daniel Knower, *The Adventures of a Forty-Niner*, 1894

*Courtesy,* Stokes Collection, The New York Public Library, New York City

Among the estimated fifteen thousand inhabitants of San Francisco were representatives of almost every nation and degree of coloring in nature. There were Germans and Frenchmen, Poles and Englishmen, hard cases from Australia and Kanakas from the Pacific islands. There were Chinese and Mexicans, Peruvians and Cubans. There were Bowery "bhoys" from New York and farm boys from Arkansas and Missouri; all caught in the dizzy optimism and endless whirl that was life in the metropolis of El Dorado.

Miners spilled into the city, coming down on the little steamers from Sacramento. They had gold in their pockets and the ague in their bones. All they asked from San Francisco was a good time. For them, the gambling rooms threw wide their doors; the saloons turned on their brightest lights. They thronged into what they called the "caffy shantangs" and spent hour after hour and ounce after ounce trying to attract the dubious favor of the women who ornamented those establishments.

Many of the miners were men of education. The character of their work, the inanity of what they were doing, reacted on their minds and made these sprees in the big city a virtual necessity. With more consciousness of the reasons for their boredom than was possessed by the farm boys and the "Pikes," they worked it off in the same ways.

Augusto Ferran and Jose Baturone were Cuban artists who had joined the procession to California. When they returned to Havana, they published a set of "Californian Types," sketched mainly in San Francisco. The picture *below*, and those on the following ten pages are from their *Album Californiano*.

A Good Freight

*Courtesy*, The New-York Historical Society, New York City

Solid Comfort

Temperance Society

Patron of the Arts

A Light Indisposition

An Excellent Segar

The Antiphlogistic System

Sightseers

Solid Arguments

Weighing the Dust

Bayard Taylor commented on the prevalence of disease among the miners he saw in San Francisco.

"A number of men who had landed only a few months before, in the fullness of hale and lusty manhood, were walking about nearly as shrunken and bloodless as the corpses they would soon become." And of one in particular, "He was sitting alone on a stone beside the water, his bare feet purple with cold on the cold, wet sand . . . He seemed unconscious of all that was passing; his long matted hair hung over his wasted face; his eyes glared steadily forward, with an expression of suffering so utterly hopeless and wild, that I shuddered at seeing it."

Both illustrations on this page are by the *courtesy* of The New-York Historical Society, New York City

Still and all, a thousand reports of golden discoveries kept the newcomers in a hopeful state of mind.

"The actual yield on most of the rivers was sufficiently encouraging. The diggers on the forks of the American, Feather and Yuba Rivers met with a steady return for their labors. On the branches of the San Joaquin, as far as the Tuolumne, the big lumps were still found. . . . The placers on Trinity River had not turned out so well as was expected and many of the miners were returning disappointed to the Sacramento."

Improved forms of the rocker or cradle were making it possible to prosper in places overlooked by miners with inadequate equipment. By the summer of 1850, the "Long Tom" was widely used —an oblong trough, usually about twelve feet in length, open at the top and at the lower end. A uniform eight inches in depth, its width increased from a foot or two at the upper end to double that width at the middle and from there to the lower end. The bottom of this broad portion was made of perforated sheet iron, curving up gradually to within two inches of the top as it approached the lower end. Under the perforations a "riffle-box" was fixed. The "tom" was set at a slight slope; the dirt was shoveled in at the upper end; water was piped or hosed in to run off at the lower end with the "tailings"; and the cleats or riffle-bars caught the gold.

When the late arrivals of 1849 reached Sacramento City on their way to the mines, a lively controversy was on between squatters who claimed to own the land on which the town was built and Captain Sutter who held a valid title to it. Compare the view of Sacramento City *below* with that shown on page 67. The building on the corner of J Street had got itself finished.

W. R. Ryan, *Personal Adventures in Upper and Lower California in 1848-49.* 1850

Some of the gold-seekers who had come by the route across the Isthmus were individualists who set off prospecting in pairs, as seen *left*.

Others retained their company organization, or joined new groups, for the march from Sacramento to the mines. (*Below*).

Both illustrations on this page are from J. M. Letts, *A Pictorial View of California.* 1853

The prosperity of the town of Stockton, (in 1848 a solitary ranch surrounded by tule marshes), was the result of its location on the way to the mines along the Mokelumne, the Stanislaus and the Tuolumne. It was the natural trading center for those booming regions, and the fortunate gentleman who had founded it sold half a million dollars worth of building lots at Stockton before the end of 1849.

The usual number of aimless loungers roamed through the canvas streets of Stockton and waited at its wharves to see the launches arrive from San Francisco. It was one of the singular phenomena of those days that, with so much work to do, there were always so many men of infinite leisure.

The roads from Stockton to the mines were filled with pack-mule trains, laden with freight. This was a much more stable business than gold mining and some of the Americans who were running the trains boasted of profits in the neighborhood of three thousand dollars a month. Profits were bounded only by the obstinacy of the mules, whose distressing habit of dying under stress of the heat, the dust and two hundred pound loads was a great sorrow to the proprietors.

This view of Stockton shows the town as it looked about midway through 1849; several months before the argonauts from Panama and Mexico would have arrived to outfit themselves for a trip up the San Joaquin.

Stockton.

William M'Ilvaine, Jr., *Sketches of Scenery and Notes of Personal Adventure in California & Mexico. 1850. Courtesy, The New York Historical Society, New York City*

Miners journeyed over the prairie (*above*) on their way from Stockton to the Tuolumne River. One of the Tuolumne camps was at Woods Creek (*below*).

Both illustrations on this page are from William M'Ilvaine, Jr., *Sketches of Scenery and Notes of Personal Adventure in California & Mexico.* 1850. *Courtesy*, The New-York Historical Society, New York City

*Kanaka Creek.*

William M'Ilvaine, Jr., *Sketches of Scenery and Notes of Personal Adventure in California & Mexico.* 1850. *Courtesy,* The New-York Historical Society, New York City

Another of the Tuolumne diggings was at Kanaka Creek, shown *above.* Swinging northward in their search for gold, over towards the Stanislaus, the late arrivals from the Isthmus might have tried their luck at South Mines. Jamestown (*below*).

*Gleason's Pictorial,* Sept. 13, 1851

W. R. Ryan, *Personal Adventures in Upper and Lower California in 1848-49.* 1850

At the Stanislaus River (*above*), one of the largest mining camps in California flourished for a time. On the banks of the river and the flank of the hill to the north of it, gold had lurked in yellow flakes and the first finders in 1848 and 1849 had made the most of it.

Shaw's Flat (*below*) was once prosperous. It lay just north of Jamestown, on the south side of the Stanislaus.

J. D. Borthwick, *Three Years in California.* 1857

"When a couple of Chinese dispute over the right to a claim, the noise and gesticulations are frightful..." So one of the Forty-Niners remarked, and the picture at the *right* illustrates the gestures if not the noise.

Frank Marryat, *Mountains and Molehills*. 1855
*Courtesy*, The New-York Historical Society, New York City

Chinese Camp (*below*) was the scene of the labors of almost five thousand industrious Celestials. Native Americans in the southern mining districts vented their spleen early on Mexicans and Frenchmen who attempted to stake out claims. But after about the middle of 1851, the Chinese came in for their share of oppression, claim-jumping and abuse.

J. D. Borthwick, *Three Years in California*. 1857

The philosophical German, whose description of San Francisco has appeared on a previous page, did most of his 1849 prospecting on the Feather River and on the American.

Life did not deal him any aces in the northern mines. Late in 1849 he made his way to Sacramento City where he worked for a while as a wood-chopper and tried, unsuccessfully, to borrow a stake from a rich fellow-German. This worthy turned out to be a Dutchman, and one who had conscientious scruples against lending money. He had no work to give; and the "rich" man's home turned out to be "a low, dirty hovel—and Mr. Swartz himself suiting the place exactly, and sitting, a great deal farther than three sheets in the wind, before a couple of bottles of most abominable gin." After this disappointment, our author paid a call at San Francisco and worked long enough in a brewery to stake a trip to Stockton and the Stanislaus.

Thirteen days after leaving Stockton, he reached Murphy's Diggings, north of the Stanislaus. "The place itself . . . consisted of one regularly-built and main street—tents, of course—with only one frame shed; but every tent a grog-shop, and in some of them gambling tables as well. Behind this street, and farther on in the flat, other tents were wildly scattered about . . . and in these the miners lived."

The sketch *below* represents Murphy's Diggings early in 1850.

Friedrich Gerstaecker, *Scenes de la Vie Californienne*. 1859

During his seven months' stay in the vicinity of Murphy's, he witnessed much of the anti-foreign agitation which was rife in the southern camps. When a murdered man was found as *above*, the cry immediately arose—"Killed by Mexicans!" And that was a good enough excuse for driving all Mexicans off their claims.

Miners' justice had odd quirks. The picture *below* shows an occurrence at Douglas Flat in the summer of 1850. A Hindu had tried to rape the wife of a California Indian. After a wild shooting session during which one Indian was killed, the Indians had demanded justice of the local *alcalde*. The court held the Hindu guilty of making trouble among the natives and allowed the Indians to administer half the lashes decreed as punishment.

Both illustrations on this page are from Friedrich Gerstaecker, *Scenes de la Vie Californienne.* 1859

# Around the Horn

ONE OF THE toughest courses ever run by sailing ships was the sea route from North Atlantic ports to San Francisco by way of Cape Horn. Under normal conditions it was a run of more than seventeen thousand miles. One hundred and thirty days sailing was regarded as a fair passage. But those gold-seekers born and bred in seaports, the sons of men who had outrun British blockades and traded from L'Orient and Havre to the hongs of China and the islands of the South Pacific, were not to be terrified by gales and high seas. Men who could name every tag of rigging and each plank in a hull would be the last to entrust their fortunes to the unknown vagaries of mules and wagons.

The Cape Horn route had been well advertised (see pages 18 and 19). Many adventurers booked single passage, but the stories of the long road by sea which have come down to us are stories of the "Companies" which banded together for the run, much as did the overland groups. There were, however, interesting points of difference.

A supposed financial advantage was one of the principal motives behind company organization for the long voyage. Many sea-going companies bought their own vessels and paid for them by subscribing cash. Each member received participating shares in return for his money. It was the belief of the promoters that the ships could be sold on arrival at San Francisco, or else used for trading ventures in the Pacific or along the coast. The return on these ventures was estimated sufficient to finance the company's mining operations, and any excess profit was to be paid as dividends to the shareholders.

Under the articles which the members of these companies signed, a strict division of labor was to be enforced on arrival at the gold regions. The men would work for the common good, and the golden yield would be divided on the basis of the number of shares held. An almost Puritan code of behavior was made obligatory on the members of the company. They sailed in most cases with the echoes of earnest farewell sermons ringing in their ears. One Boston company was given a handsomely-bound pulpit Bible as a collective gift at parting, and in addition each man received a small Bible. With these went the admonition that the members "were going to a far country where all were in ignorance and sin." The men were told that it was their duty to go with the Bible in one hand and their good New England civilization in the other; thereby to conquer wickedness and implant their principles on the soil of California.

Alas and alack! Stout ships were already going begging at San Francisco—the days of the coastwise trade were over—sick men and idle men could not or would not do their share of work—and the highest principles were not always proof against the social conditions to be found in the mining camps. Yet the monotonous and often trying voyage in crowded ships taught lessons of self-reliance and self-control to the stouter-fibred. When the disappointments and failures encountered at journey's end broke up and dissipated the companies, many individuals rose out of the wreck to win success and leave their mark on the law, the politics or the commercial life of the emerging state.

Meanwhile, the enrolled members of sea-going companies sat impatiently in their club-rooms and consumed mountains of tobacco while waiting for their ships to be bought, made ready and provisioned. Few of them foresaw the chancy and dismal future. They pored over maps and charts, and books on the various processes used in mining. They recalled to mind everything their grandfathers had had to say about the China trade. They disputed endlessly and aroused one another's golden hopes.

The earlier venturers around the Horn made the best bargains they could in a booming market for well-found ships. Their infection with gold-fever did not, however, seriously affect their judgment of seaworthiness nor their caution in shipping competent officers and crews. One company enrolled as seamen more than a dozen men who had served as mates aboard other vessels.

William Sidney Mount's painting "California News," *below*, was executed at the height of the excitement. It portrays a group in a Long Island post office as they listen to the latest word from El Dorado. There is no better contemporary record of the fascination which the great adventure exercised on all kinds and conditions of Americans.

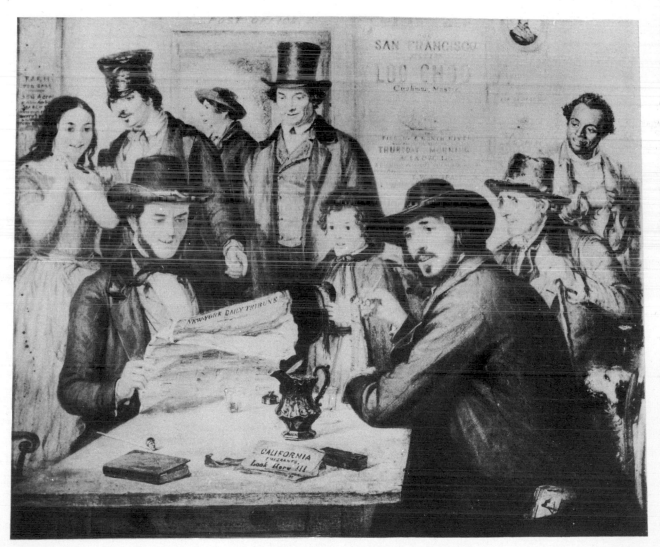

*Courtesy*, Mr. and Mrs. Ward Melville, and The Suffolk Museum, Stony Brook, L. I., N. Y.

# WEIGH ANCHOR!

*Courtesy,* Beverly Historical Society, Beverly, Mass.

The barque *San Francisco* (*above*) sailed on August 15, 1849, from Beverly, Massachusetts, bound for California. She carried the forty members of the "Beverly Joint Stock San Francisco Company," a steward, a cook, twenty pigs, a kitten, a dog and a crow.

Seventy-six days out of port, the *San Francisco* rounded Cape Horn in "strong gales and a heavy sea." From there on to California, she made good way despite "rolling gunnels under and the salt water smashing across the decks"; for she arrived safely in San Francisco harbor only one hundred and forty-nine days out of Beverly.

Regardless of the success or failure of the gold-seekers aboard her, the planed boards, building bricks and house-frames carried as cargo made the *San Francisco's* voyage a profitable one; for she was small enough to sail up river to Sacramento and unload in the middle of the housing boom in progress there. Nor did her ribs rot in harbor. She sailed home again to Beverly.

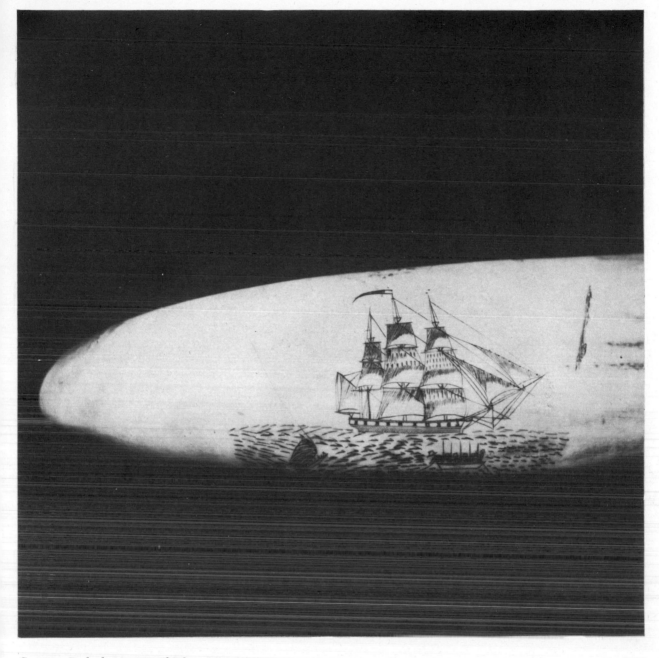

*Courtesy*, Peabody Museum of Salem, Mass.

The ship *Elizabeth* (her picture *above*, in scrimshaw on a whale's tooth, commemorates her first employment as a whaler) sailed from Salem, Massachusetts, on April 5, 1849. She carried the "Salem Mining Company" safely to San Francisco in one hundred and sixty-five days. The voyage was somewhat unfortunate, although the twelve members of the Company praised Captain Kimball's skill and tact.

Intense cold off Patagonia disturbed the passengers; for a twenty-day period, the vessel lay becalmed. And on arrival at San Francisco one of the disappointed gold-seekers noted: "The most contemptible dirty place one could wish to see. Not fit for man or beast." The rest is silence, so far as the "Salem Mining Company" is concerned.

The *Elizabeth* shared the fate of most dull-sailing ships—a permanent berth on the flats in San Francisco harbor. After use for some time as a store ship, she ended her career in a dignified manner as a U. S. Bonded Warehouse. Abandoned vessels littered the banks of the river at Sacramento and rotted away in Stockton Slough as well. Only smart schooners fit for trade to Hawaii, and the steam-launches carried out as deck cargo by some of the gold rush ships, found willing purchasers on the Pacific coast.

Before they took up their stations on the run between Panama City and San Francisco, the steamships of the Pacific Mail Company had made the trip around the Horn. The *Senator* sailed from New York on March 10, 1849; she is shown *above* in an oil painting by James and John Bard. *Below* is a lithograph of the *Tennessee*. She left New York on December 6, 1849, and broke up after running ashore in Bolinas Bay on March 6, 1853.

These first trips out were rather risky. The captain of the *Oregon* had to clap irons on most of his crew to keep them from jumping ship at San Francisco. As ever, there was much complaint about steamship food: "The pork is rusty, the beef rotten, the duff half-cooked and the beans contain two bugs to a bean," reported one dissatisfied passenger.

Both illustrations on this page are by the *courtesy* of The Mariners' Museum, Newport News, Va.

Because the Californian excitement continued without let-up, shipbuilders were encouraged to design and produce vessels whose speed, and ability to work in light winds and across belts of calm, guaranteed swift passage to El Dorado. These ships were the extreme "California Clippers"—queens of the sea between 1850 and 1855, so long as passenger traffic covered their deficiencies as cargo carriers and the high wages paid their crews.

Still, regardless of their defects and the motives of their building, sky-scraping masts, sharp hulls and spread of sail combined to make the clipper ship one of the loveliest of American inventions.

The sailing notice at the *right* refers to the *R. B. Forbes* pictured *below*. Samuel Hall built her at East Boston in 1851.

GLIDDEN & WILLIAMS' LINE
—FOR—

SAN FRANCISCO

TO SAIL ON OR BEFORE    *Thursday, Aug. 22*

☞ FROM LEWIS WHARF. ☜

THE CELEBRATED EXTREME CLIPPER SHIP

R. B. FORBES

J. C. BALLARD.........COMMANDER.

This is one of the fastest ships afloat, as the following passages testify :

Boston to Honolulu in - - 96 1-2 days.
Boston to Batavia in - - -75    "
Padang to Boston in - - -75    "

☞She will take no freight after her advertised day,    shippers will please note.

*For Freight or Passage, apply at*

The California Packet Office,

No. 114......State Street.

☞To be followed by the Famous Extreme Clipper Ships
"*West Wind,*" & "*Ringleader.*"

Watson, Pr.

*Courtesy*, Peabody Museum of Salem, Mass.

*Gleason's Pictorial*, Nov. 8. 1851

*Gleason's Pictorial*, May 10, 1851

Steamships were a long time catching up with the records made by the clippers.

The *Flying Cloud* (at *left* as she was being launched at Donald McKay's shipyard) set the record for the run from New York to San Francisco—a record broken only by herself in 1854.

Captain Josiah Perkins Creesy (*right*) was a "driving" skipper. Grinnell, Minturn and Company, of New York, chose him to take out the *Flying Cloud* on her maiden voyage, knowing full well that Creesy would try for the record.

Spars carried away; sails blew out; the mainmast cracked under the strains; but Captain Creesy bore down hard on his crew. On August 31, 1851, only eighty-nine days and a few hours from home port, the anchor was let go in the harbor of San Francisco.

*Courtesy*, Peabody Museum of Salem, Mass.

The *Flying Cloud* is shown at the *left*, as she looked just before her departure on the record run.

*Gleason's Pictorial*, May 31, 1851

*Gleason's Pictorial,* June 7, 1851

The term "clipper" did not apply to the rig of a ship or to its size, but to the vessel's ability to run swiftly—to "clip." The *Mermaid,* for example, was barque-rigged (*above*): she was about one-third the size of the *Flying Cloud.*

The *Telegraph* (shown *below* as work was being completed on her hull) was intended for service as a California packet. Her lines were considered fast but dangerous.

*Gleason's Pictorial,* June 14, 1851

The portrait at the *left* was taken some years after Captain Robert Waterman's famous 1851 voyage in the clipper *Challenge*, but his face still shows much of the resolution and force that made him in his prime one of the greatest master mariners in our history.

He had already left the sea and settled near what is today the town of Fairfield, California, when the Griswolds of New York asked him to take command of the *Challenge*. (She is shown *below*, in W. H. Webb's New York yard, where she was built).

Her maiden voyage to San Francisco has been described as "a classic instance of a voyage in an American 'Hell Ship.'" Nine members of the crew died; the chief mate narrowly escaped being murdered; Captain Waterman stood trial for murder on the high seas; and all in an unsuccessful attempt to set a record.

*Courtesy*, Peabody Museum of Salem, Mass.

*Gleason's Pictorial*, June 21, 1851

With everything set that could draw, the clipper *Syren* passes Boston Light, bound for California —another of the 1851 crop of fleet voyagers to the gold country.

*Gleason's Pictorial*, July 5, 1851

On July 5, 1851, the *Union*, a steamship, ran aground on the coast of Lower California. Vapors of the previous day's celebration still fogged the brains of the crew, and the result was the catastrophe shown *below*—a sad commentary on excessive patriotism.

*Courtesy*, The Mariners' Museum, Newport News, Va.

U. S. STEAMER GOLDEN GATE.

Charles B. Stuart, *The Naval & Mail Steamers of the United States.* 1853

The fate of the *Union* did not depress Messrs. Howland and Aspinwall unduly. Those astute ship operators had the *Golden Gate* fitted out at Webb's New York yard in plenty of time to replace the wrecked vessel on the run between Panama City and San Francisco. As may be seen *above*, the *Golden Gate* carried sail enough to justify the advertisements that the wind "would bring her to a safe port, should her machinery give out."

Meanwhile foreign vessels continued to carry thousands of Frenchmen, Germans, Englishmen, either direct to San Francisco or to American ports wherefrom the overland routes might easily be reached. Despite the Foreign Miners' Tax and other less legal obstructions put in the way of European and South American enterprise—("In general, California justice favors the Americans at the expense of foreigners," as one Frenchman put it)—the gold-seekers from afar were not a bit discouraged.

As indicated on this page, the rage for emigration was not confined to western Europe. In Russia, Sweden and Poland, the year 1850 saw publication of guides to the gold fields, a little better contrived than the 1849 crop but effecting a like result.

*Courtesy,* The Bancroft Library, University of California, Berkeley, Calif.

G. Blok, *Brief Geographical-Statistical Description of California.* 1850. *Courtesy,* The Stanford University Libraries, Stanford, Calif.

*Courtesy,* The Bancroft Library, University of California, Berkeley, Calif.

The sound of the caulker's mallet was loud all through 1852 and 1853, as building yards continued to turn out ships for the California passage. Architects and owners were proud of their towering vessels. Many were commemorated in oil paintings. The *Herald of the Morning* was in service on the Cape Horn run from 1853 to 1887, and her portrait *above* is attributed to J. W. Stancliff.

Nathaniel Currier saw opportunity in the popular enthusiasm for clippers and turned out a series of ship prints. The Currier print *below* shows the *Young America.*

Both illustrations on this page are by the *courtesy* of The Mariners' Museum, Newport News, Va.

The clipper ship voyages around the Horn were fundamentally business propositions, but the American tendency to turn practical concerns into sporting ventures gave an almost boyish zest to the competition for record passages. A three-thousand-dollar bonus awaited the skipper who made the Cape Horn voyage in under a hundred days. Huge bets were placed on favorite ships to arrive ahead of a designated time. Loud was the lamentation when fog or a belt of calm interfered with a record run.

Clipper ship captains were as aware of their responsibilities to the sporting fraternity as were the Mississippi River captains who raced for records with their safety-valves lashed down. Sail was cracked on from anchor to anchor, as much as a vessel would carry without "pulling the sticks out of her." On one occasion, with twenty thousand dollars in bets at stake, Captain Philip Dumaresq of the *Surprise* reefed topsails only twice between Sandy Hook and San Francisco, and took the vessel into harbor by himself, through a thick blanket of fog. Time—ninety-six days!

In the picture *below* (an oil painting attributed to J. E. Butterworth), the *Comet* is seen in a hurricane off Bermuda, one of the hazards of the Cape Horn route. This incident took place on October 2, 1852, and Currier published a handsome lithograph of it. The print was in all probability based on this painting.

*Courtesy*, The Mariners' Museum, Newport News, Va.

*Rio de Janeiro Pitoresco. Courtesy,* The New York Public Library, New York City

The average gold-seeker from the United States was used to thinking of all foreign things and peoples as immeasurably inferior to their analogues in his own blessed country. He received an educational shock when his ship chanced to touch at South American ports.

Rio de Janeiro was the first great city encountered to the southward. The men from Yankeeland found its harbor thronged with trading ships. Its landing stage (*above*) was ringed about with impressive buildings. It was not Boston, and it was not New York, but it was exotic and beautiful and deeply disturbing to prejudice.

The inhabitants of Rio, for their part, were not altogether unprejudiced. They had heard stories of the North Americans. Consequently, when the earliest group of gold rush ships put in at Rio, the Brazilians thought they were transporting lawless American filibusters, intent on overturning the government.

After leaving Rio de Janeiro, few California-bound vessels touched at any port until Cape Horn had been doubled. In theory, time could be saved by avoiding the passage around the Cape and sailing through, either the Straits of Le Maire south of Tierra del Fuego, or the much more difficult Straits of Magellan. It was generally believed, however, that ships of any size would be better advised to go around the Horn. For all the moans and groans of scared and seasick gold hunters, miserable in their bunks, the days of storm and stress off the Cape were to be preferred to the adverse winds and erratic currents encountered in a passage of the Straits from east to west.

A typical clipper log-book entry describes the rounding of Cape Horn as follows:

*"July 12. Latitude 55° 27' 00" Longitude 65° 15' 00" Winds, south Wore ship to SE at noon & wind died away gradually & at 10 P M hauled to SW & Midnight to West. At 2 A M calm and remained so till 8 A M we took a wind from NW which came on very fiery & we furled Royal staysails and topgallant sails & at noon put 2 reefs in the topsails. We saw 1 Ship and 2 Barques this forenoon bound to NE. The sea was quite smooth at 8 A M but a large sea on at noon. Cape Horn at noon bore true North of us. 47 days 16 hours from New York."*

The picture *below* of an unidentified ship rounding Cape Horn in a squall was another popular subject "done on stone" by Currier and Ives.

*Courtesy*, The Mariners' Museum, Newport News, Va.

*Courtesy*, The Mariners' Museum, Newport News, Va.

Ports of call on the western coast of South America were even more of a revelation to American emigrants than Rio had been. Talcahuano on the Chilean coast, the island of Juan Fernandez, or the city of Valparaiso (*above*, as the Forty-Niners saw it) were conventional stops for water and supplies.

Valparaiso was gay with wide plazas and music and entertainment; a most attractive city to men who tumbled ashore after weeks at sea. Some excessively Yankee voyagers, however, wrote home sour and vaguely wistful references to the sinful conditions prevailing in the Latin republics. Sabbath-breaking was particularly noted.

Many northward-faring ships put in at Callao, the port of Lima, Peru. But the gold-seekers aboard them were now in spirit sniffing the air of California; they were anxious for an end to sight-seeing and wonder; they wanted to feel the gold dust between their fingers. When a vessel stopped at Acapulco (*above*), or Mazatlan (*below*), to pick up bedraggled veterans of the trails across Mexico, the men who had come round the Horn were resentful and showed it. Especially were they outraged when becalmed north of the Line. One clipper captain, rolling idly under the tropic sun, lowered his boat and pulled around the ship "in hopes by so doing to raise a breese."

Both illustrations on this page are from J. R. Bartlett, *Personal Narrative of Explorations*. 1854

# THROUGH THE GOLDEN GATE

*"Perfectly calm and no steerage way till 9 P M we took a faint air from South which lasted the remainder of the night & about 4:30 A M we saw a light on the telegraph house & at daylight were about equidistant from the Farralones bearing NW true & Lobos Point NE true. Soon after took a pilot, remained calm till 9 A M when we took a breeze and passed between the heads of San Francisco . . ."*

Through 1851 and 1852, log entries, like the one just quoted, noted the arrival of thousands of vessels at San Francisco. That cosmopolitan city took the sea-voyagers to its capacious bosom, just as it had received the men of the overland trails down from the mines, or the hopefuls who had crossed Mexico or the Isthmus. Early arrivals by ship had landed in the teeming tent city described in previous chapters. But the clipper ship passengers found that the character of life in San Francisco was changing month by month, as the more responsible among the citizens built up a framework of law and society. San Francisco markets were no longer so subject to periodic famines and gluts. Businessmen were able to make proper arrangement for shipments by regular steamer mail, and the clippers were setting a fine record for speed and regularity of delivery. Until the railroad bridged the continent, one of the institutions of San Francisco's commerce was "steamer day." Collections were made; correspondence set in order; special editions of the newspapers were run off; the manifold details of the import trade, so vital in the economy of the city, were arranged; all subject to the fortnightly departure of a steamship for Panama City.

As order came in the business life of the city, it became obvious that something would have to be done about the uproarious part of the population, the predatory gangs, foreign adventurers and other blacklegs who had been tolerated in the first flush times. Even before President Fillmore signed the bill which admitted California to the Union, San Francisco had formed a city government, weak enough in all truth, but indicative of a desire for municipal order. After all, the city represented California to the world; there came the ships, the traders, the immigrants. In 1849, popular justice had caught up with the "Hounds," a body of New York vagabonds who preyed on the Chileans and Peruvians; but occasional forays against crime availed very little. The city government was powerless to do more than threaten. Not until 1851 did the hoodlums, pickpockets and murderers who lurked in "Sydney Town" (as the district along the upper part of Pacific Street had come to be called) get a real taste of law.

Gambling houses continued prosperous. Miners still rolled into town for a good time. Saloons did not diminish. But churches and charitable associations began to flourish as well; schools and "culture" societies came into being. Sidewalks were built; the roadways were rescued from primeval mud; the old Cove was filled in, and children carried flowers through the streets on "May Walks." The great fires of 1851 were only temporary setbacks to the material prosperity of the city; its spirit they did not affect for a moment.

*Courtesy,* Stokes Collection, The New York Public Library

In the early lithographic view of San Francisco *above*, the ship *Philadelphia* is shown afire. This vessel burned on June 24, 1849, a fact which would appear to establish the date of the view. A second state of this print exists, in which signs have been added to a number of the buildings.

The original painting by Henry Firks, from which this print was made, is the property of the Newport, R. I., Historical Society and shows interesting variations from the print.

This picture, and the one on page 132, may stand for the San Francisco which the first voyagers by sea experienced—the little community so soon to be scourged by fire and water, to be swamped by lawlessness and vice, to fall and to rise grander than before. "I expected to take up either the ministry or law," one man wrote home, "but there is neither law nor gospel here and yet it is most orderly."

*Courtesy,* Stokes Collection, The New York Public Library

The water-color view of San Francisco *above* dates from about the beginning of 1850. It is reproduced as an example of native art of the period, and for all its faults gives a vivid idea of the congestion of shipping. The lithograph *below,* also a native production, pictures the jubilation in Portsmouth Square on October 29, 1850, when San Francisco celebrated the admission of California to the Federal Union.

*Courtesy,* The Huntington Library, San Marino, Calif.

*Gleason's Pictorial*, May 3, 1851

Popular magazines of the day "featured" the new metropolis of California. The 1851 view *above* shows San Francisco "drawn on the spot from the foot of Telegraph Hill." Three weeks later, the same magazine ran the sketch *below* which shows "the upper side of Montgomery Street, at the foot of Washington," and tried for a little local color in its caption by adding that the street was "crowded by *hombres* in every imaginable costume."

*Gleason's Pictorial*, May 24, 1851

A London lithographer produced this handsome view of the city after a sketch by S. F. Marryat, dated 1851.

Alonzo Delano, *Pen Knife Sketches; or, Chips of the Old Block.* 1853. *Courtesy*, The Library of Congress, Washington, D. C.

The condition of the streets in San Francisco was still the subject of continuous and somewhat wearisome jest. The Chinese in the sketch *above* was having some trouble with the wooden planking which did duty for sidewalk and roadway.

The Niantic Hotel, seen in the waterfront view *below*, had been built on the hull of an abandoned vessel, the *Niantic*, and stood about where Clay and Sansome Streets intersect.

Frank Marryat, *Mountains and Molehills.* 1855. *Courtesy*, The New-York Historical Society, New York City

These contemporary sketches of amusements at San Francisco give some idea of the wide diversity offered the bored man with a bag of dust.

J. D. Borthwick, *Three Years in California*. 1857.

Above *right* is a bull and bear fight. The picture *below* shows the "second bar" at one of the Portsmouth Square gambling houses, where, incredibly enough, were served "tea, coffee, chocolate and similar beverages, with preserves and pastry . . . at this table a young lady waits in a black silk dress, looking smilingly upon you when you ask for something, and stared at by the b'hoys when they come down from the mines."

Friedrich Gerstaecker, *Scenes de la Vie Californienne*. 1859

Most San Franciscans had come to believe that disastrous fires which raged through the city early in 1851 were the work of arsonists from "Sydney Town." A citizens' committee which numbered, among others, Stephen Payran, W. T. Coleman and Sam Brannan, the former Mormon elder who knew sin when he saw it, took the law into its own hands and formed the first Vigilance Committee. The city government protested in vain, for its record of inaction was too flagrant.

Spurred on by the city's leading newspaper, the *Alta California*, more than eight hundred merchants and bankers (lawyers were specifically excluded from membership) began a glorious clean-up—patrolling the streets, arresting suspects, and searching houses for stolen goods.

*Courtesy,* California Historical Society, San Francisco, Calif.

In the daguerreotype *above,* the standing figure is the Hon. Edward Gilbert, senior editor of the *Alta.* Gilbert's career in journalism ended in 1852, when his bitter criticism of General J. W. Denver brought him death on the duelling ground. The seated figure is E. C. Kemble, Gilbert's associate on the paper. A certificate of membership in the first Vigilance Committee is reproduced *below.*

*Courtesy,* The New-York Historical Society, New York City

*Courtesy*, The Huntington Library, San Marino, Calif.

At two o'clock in the morning of Wednesday, June 11, 1851, the newly-formed Vigilance Committee took, tried and hanged John Jenkins, an Australian thief from "Sydney Town." The strength of the popular movement overawed any attempts at rescue. The crude lithograph of the execution *above* is first-hand reporting, sketched on the spot and published in San Francisco. This is true also of the lithograph *below*, which shows the execution of Whittaker and McKenzie, two more Sydney Ducks who stayed to brazen out the storm. This, the last official action of the first Vigilance Committee, took place in August. Its example, despite the best efforts of the Governor, of Sheriff Jack Hays, and a writ of *habeas corpus* to hold the men for trial in a regular court, sent most of the remaining scoundrels hustling out of town.

*Courtesy*, The New-York Historical Society, New York City

These two daguerreotypes were made some time in 1852, according to our best information. The view *above* shows the "water-front lots," an area now comprising most of the financial district below Montgomery Street. Telegraph Hill provides the background for the picture *below*.

Both illustrations on this page are by the *courtesy* of the California Historical Society, San Francisco, Calif.

# First Decade

THE DAYS of Forty-Nine, considered as a social phenomenon, did not come to a term when the placers ceased to yield and there were fewer rich chances for the single miner or the wandering pair of "pardners." Nor did they end in 1854, when the easy years of disorder, speculation and high-living climaxed; when the tide of immigration began to ebb, and when the world began to realize that fortunes could be won in California only on the same hard terms as elsewhere.

The financial depression of 1855 ended many bright hopes and swallowed up much wealth that luck and labor had wrested out of the rich earth. Many one-time miners took up farm land. Others who failed to find "even the color" in their pans returned to the home towns from which they had set out with high hopes and boastful words. And still one could not say that the great adventure had come to an end.

The old free-and-easy independence of life in the gold rush days deteriorated into license and abuse, became insolent, and brought down on itself the wrath of the "better element" during 1856. Amid general approval, the reign of law and order was instituted by illegal but understandable means. As society began to stratify, the bonds of convention began to tighten and conduct became more decorous. Californian industry, by 1858, was no longer an uproarious, single-minded search for El Dorado; for as the commercial life of the state revived, the economic structure was reared on broader bases, and new industries and occupations came to the fore. In the great march of time, the accidental facts of the gold rush dwindled in importance and disappeared, but its spirit and symbolism remained. It is even yet an immortal American memory; a tale told by fathers to sons; a legend of high heroism and laughter in adversity, from which the darker elements have long since been purged away.

No less does the gold rush survive in the permanent impress it left on the character of California and Californians. In the spirit of the pioneers, the people of the state have always taken pride in their ability to accept troubles as healthy challenges to head and hand. Just as the Forty-Niners looked to qualities proved on the trails and deserts, in flood and fire, for their measure of a man, so Californians of later times tend to judge their fellows by man-standards rather than by the accidents of birth or bank-account. They have never lost the awareness of special character, so well expressed by one of the pioneers:

"The world, you know, is composed generally of three classes—good, bad and indifferent. But California is an exception to this rule. I haven't made up my mind whether it always formed a component part of the earth, or whether it is an offshoot of some comet that dropped into this spot by the law of gravitation. California is either very good or very bad. The soil is very wet or very dry, the land is very high or very low, the people very good or very bad. It is either percussion or squib, and but small chance for indifferent. If you get a farm, it will be No. 1 or No. 0. If you go into business, it will be good or good for nothing."

## MINERS AND MINES

Up in the diggings, as in the earliest days of the gold excitement, the true-blooded prospector was still ready to drop whatever he had in hand to follow new flashes of the golden gleam—as far north as the shadow of Shasta, or southward to Mariposa, or wherever rumor ran. An early example of this restlessness, one that may stand for all, was the "Gold Lake" hoax of 1850. Alonzo Delano, in his settlement on Feather River, watched its early stages.

"A wonderful lake had been discovered, a hundred miles back among the mountains, towards the head of the Middle Fork of Feather River, the shores of which abounded with gold, and to such an extent that it lay like pebbles on the beach. An extraordinary ferment among the people ensued, and a grand rush was made from the towns in search of this splendid El Dorado. Stores were left to take care of themselves, business of all kinds was dropped, mules were suddenly bought up at exorbitant prices, and crowds started off to search for the golden lake."

Although the exodus ruined a promising town-lot speculation for Delano, he was philosophical enough to note that the country was more perfectly explored after this swarm through the mountains.

Among the gullible prospectors who went looking for Gold Lake were two former acquaintances: Captain J. Goldsborough Bruff (see pages 57 to 59) and Pete Lassen. In the picture *below*, sketched near Honey Lake in October, 1850, Bruff is shown seated beside the tree. Lassen is sleeping beside Bruff, his arm over his head.

*Courtesy,* The Huntington Library, San Marino, Calif.

The fate of many № 8

From Original Drawing by J. G. Bruff. *Courtesy,* The W. R. Coe Collection, Yale University Library

In the gloomy little drawing *above,* Captain Bruff summarized his opinion of the whole adventure, Gold Lake included.

Other and later adventurers were not at all discouraged by repeated failure. In the picture *below,* a stagecoach climbs past laboring miners, its hopeful passengers lending the animals a shoulder on the road to some new strike. Before the formation of the California Stage Company by James E. Birch and Frank Stevens in 1859, dozens of companies were competing for the business at rates that left only a tiny profit for their proprietors.

Alonzo Delano, *Pen Knife Sketches; or, Chips of the Old Block.* 1853. *Courtesy,* The Library of Congress, Washington, D. C.

STARTING.

THE END OF THE MULE

Lith. & Pub.ᵈ by B

Californians were willing to laugh at their own disappointments, as this early cartoon proves.

NOT EVEN THE COLOUR

RETURNING.

& Rey San Francisco.

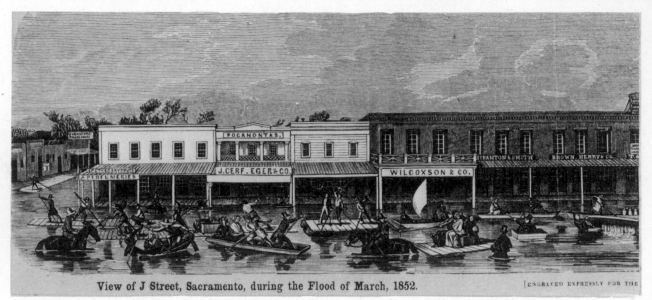

View of J Street, Sacramento, during the Flood of March, 1852.

*Courtesy,* Edward Eberstadt & Sons, New York City

It was not easy, however, to laugh off the trials by water and fire which Sacramento City under-went in 1852.

VIEW OF THE FIRE IN SACRAMENTO CITY
on the night of 2 & 3 of November 1852. Taken from the Levee.
LOSS; TEN MILLIONS OF DOLLARS!!!

*Courtesy,* The California State Library, Sacramento, Calif.

Notable in the early Fifties were the great changes that had come about in mining methods; developments which would secure the productiveness of the older placers for more years than the sluice-boxes and "long toms" could guarantee. Nor were these gains solely economic. Because construction of flumes, by which water could be brought up from the canyons or across valleys to the sluices, required concentration of capital and effort, the individualistic spirit began to die out among the miners. River-bed mining, in which mountain torrents were turned out of their natural channels during summer, so that the gold in the bed might be gathered before the rainy season set in, was a long, expensive and chancy operation. Its success demanded close co-operation and hard labor on the part of those who banded together to engage in it. This was no work for amateurs.

A flume for river-bed mining had to be of sufficient capacity to carry the whole amount of water that ran in the river. Standing waist-deep in the icy current, the miners piled boulders up to make a dam which would slant the running stream into the wooden flume. As a rule, a second line of rocks was built behind the first, and the space between them filled up with clayey soil.

Water wheels were erected across the flume, so that the motion of the prisoned river might be used to pump out what water was left in the former bed of the stream. The picture *below* shows a flume, with water wheels at work on the Yuba River.

J. D. Borthwick, *Three Years in California.* 1857

These sketches of the newer methods in use for mining were made in the fall of 1853. *Above* is a claim on Horse Shoe Bar, in the North Fork of the American River. The wheel was used for pumping out water on back claims. The flume at Parks' Bar on the Yuba is shown *below*.

Both illustrations on this page are from *Gleason's Pictorial*, Mar. 25, 1854

*Courtesy,* The California State Library, Sacramento, Calif.

The 1854 copy of J. M. Hutchings' "Miners' Ten Commandments" *above* differs in very small details from the original issue of 1853. Considerable social history may be deduced from the text. Note the ubiquitous Elephant, the symbol of what a man went out to see.

*Courtesy*, E. B. Crocker Art Gallery, Sacramento, Calif.

Charles Nahl, painter of "Sunday Morning in the Mines" (*above*), and of "Fandango" (see page 1), came to San Francisco from Paris in 1850. He worked as a miner at Rough and Ready Camp in Nevada County during 1851.

Nahl lost his earliest sketches of mining society in the great Sacramento fire of 1852, but he could draw on a well-stocked memory for material when he illustrated Delano's *Pen Knife Sketches* and *Old Block's Sketch-Book,* and when in the early Eighteen-Seventies he undertook these canvases.

G.H.Goddard del.

Entered according to act of Congress in the year 1852
Northern

SO

Ja

*Courtesy,* The California State Library, Sacramento, Calif.

Sonora boasted in 1851 that it contained more gamblers, drunkards and fast women, and more and larger lumps of gold than any place of equal size west of the Sierra. Gold had been found at Sonora in the summer of 1848 by a party of Mexicans, and the first name given these diggings was "Sonorian Camp."

In March, 1850, a group of Mexican miners, forced off their claims at Sonora by true-born citizens of the United States, struck it rich at a site a few miles north of their former location. Philanthropic Americans, who felt that so much prosperity would be bad for the Mexicans,

persuaded them to leave, and began to work the diggings themselves. First called "Hildreth's Diggings," the place was renamed for a short space "American Camp." At last it became Columbia—Gem of the Southern Mines!

VIEW OF AGUA FRIA VALLEY.

No spot on the Californian earth was too small to be commemorated in native art. During the early Fifties, local artists distributed their work in lithography, as executed in the San Francisco shops of Justh, Quirot and Company, or Britton and Rey. No longer was California dependent for popular art on the Saronys, Curriers and Endicotts of Boston and New York.

SPRINGFIELD, TUOLUMNE COUNTY.
Published by G. S. Wells, Sonora. May 1853

Both illustrations on this page are by the *courtesy* of Edward Eberstadt & Sons, New York City

*Courtesy*, Editor in Chief

The date of the view of Sutter's Mill *above* is conjectural. The costume of the gentleman stand-ing in the foreground does not give the reader much help.

Conceivably, this picture may belong to the series of views shown on the next five pages. An unknown daguerreotypist made them in 1852, and they were originally in the archives of the Cali-fornia State Division of Mines. If, as may be presumed, they were made during some primeval survey or other, they were without doubt the subject of much legislative growling about "waste of the taxpayers' money." As matters stand, they constitute a unique record of the times, and the historian is beholden to the unknown artist.

## SPANISH FLAT, 1852

Spanish Flat (not to be confused with Spanish Diggings) lay about midway between Placerville and Georgetown—a few miles east of Coloma.

IN AUBURN RAVINE, 1852

*Courtesy,* The California State Library, Sacramento, Calif.

As early as the summer of 1848, Rich Dry Diggings across the North Fork of the American River was yielding eight hundred to fifteen thousand dollars a day per man to the fortunate gold seekers who settled there. Some poetically-minded veteran of the trails was moved by the beauty of the view to give the place a new name, and so it became Auburn.

By 1852, a series of flumes had been built to bring water to claims which no longer yielded, and a second time of prosperity came to Auburn.

## HEAD OF AUBURN RAVINE, 1852

*Courtesy*, The California State Library, Sacramento, Calif.

Four miles east of Grass Valley, the banks and gravel slopes of Deer Creek had yielded nobly in 1849. By March, 1850, Deer Creek Dry Diggings grew to be a town of over ten thousand inhabitants, and its name had become Nevada City. John Mackay and James Fair were one-time citizens, men whose names live on in the story of the Comstock Lode. George Hearst made a stake there which was the foundation of his fortunes.

## NEVADA CITY, CALA., 1852

*Courtesy*, The California State Library, Sacramento, Calif.

Fire and flood racked Nevada City—its placers ceased to yield—but in December, 1852, the little town was host to a council of miners which met to formulate rules and regulations for quartz mining. This code, drawn up with the aid of William Morris Stewart, determined ownership of a claim all along the dips, spurs and angles of the vein, rather than by area above ground.

In 1854 and 1855, Nevada City was the scene of "Madame Moustache's" early and successful operations at the *vingt-et-un* table. This celebrated lady-gambler, born Eleanore Dumont, was plump, French and a most adroit specialist in male psychology. Her great days were spent in Nevada City. There she returned, years afterward, broken and old.

NEAR NEVADA CITY, 1852

*Courtesy,* The California State Library, Sacramento, Calif.

The hard-working men in the view *above* do not exhibit any Chesterfieldian characteristics—nonetheless, by 1852, a "society" in the limited sense was developing in the camps.

The robust amusements of the early days were still popular, but a prejudice had sprung up against professional gamblers and notorious trouble-makers. The group of formal invitations on the facing page is an indication of the settling process which was at work.

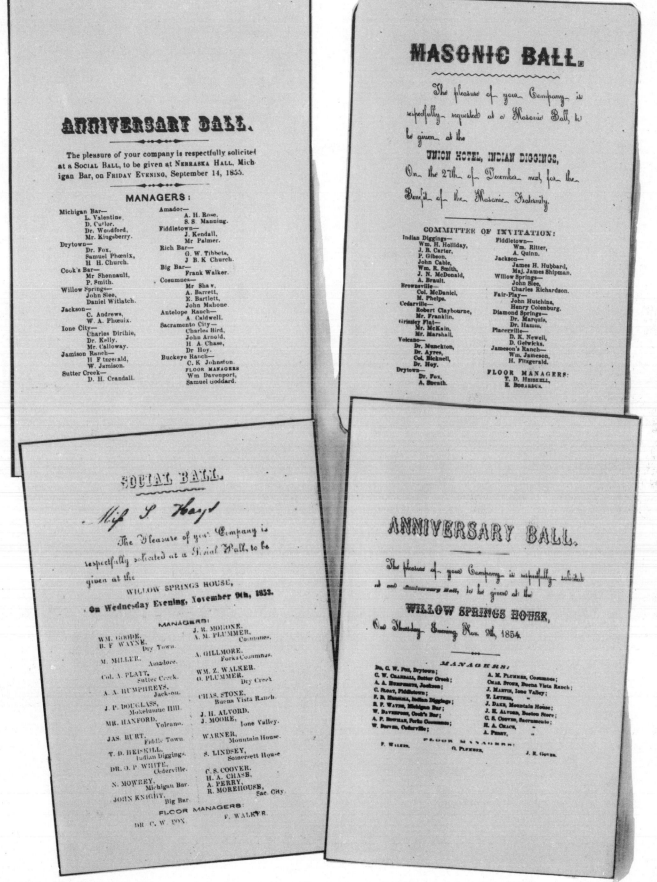

## ANNIVERSARY BALL.

The pleasure of your company is respectfully solicited at a Social Ball, to be given at Nebraska Hall, Michigan Bar, on Friday Evening, September 14, 1855.

### MANAGERS:

Michigan Bar—
L. Valentine,
D. Cutler,
Dr. Woodford,
Mr. Kingsberry.
Drytown—
Dr. Fox,
Samuel Phœnix,
H. H. Church.
Cook's Bar—
Mr Shennault,
P. Smith.
Willow Springs—
John Slee,
Daniel Witlatch.
Jackson—
C. Andrews,
W. A. Phœnix.
Ione City—
Charles Dirhie,
Dr. Kelly,
Mr. Calloway.
Jamison Ranch—
H F tzgerald,
W. Jamison.
Sutter Creek—
D. H. Crandall.

Amador—
A. H. Rose,
S.S. Manning.
Fiddletown—
J. Kendall,
Mr Palmer.
Rich Bar—
G. W. Tibbets,
J B.K Church.
Big Bar—
Frank Walker.
Cosumnes—
Mr Sha v,
A. Barrett,
E. Bartlett,
John Mahone.
Antelope Ranch—
A. Caldwell.
Sacramento City—
Charles Bird,
John Arnold,
H A. Chase,
Dr Hoy.
Buckeye Ranch—
C. K. Johnston.
FLOOR MANAGERS
Wm Davenport,
Samuel Goddard.

## MASONIC BALL.

The pleasure of your Company is respectfully requested at a Masonic Ball, to be given at the

### UNION HOTEL, INDIAN DIGGINGS,

On the 27th of December next for the Benefit of the Masonic Fraternity.

### COMMITTEE OF INVITATION:

Indian Diggings—
Wm. H. Holliday,
J. R. Carter,
F. Gibson,
John Cable,
Wm. R. Smith,
J. N. McDonald,
A. Brault.
Brownsville—
Col. McDaniel,
M. Phelps.
Cedarville—
Robert Claybourne,
Mr. Franklin.
Grizzley Flat—
Mr. McKain,
Mr. Marshall.
Volcano—
Dr. Munckton,
Dr. Ayres,
Col. Bicknell,
Dr. Hoy.
Drytown—
Dr. Fox,
A. Swaith.

Fiddletown—
Wm. Ritter,
A. Quinn.
Jackson—
James H. Hubbard,
Maj. James Shipman.
Willow Springs—
John Slee,
Charles Richardson.
Fair-Play—
John Hutchins,
Henry Colenburg.
Diamond Springs—
Dr. Marquis,
Dr. Hamm.
Placerville—
D. K. Newell,
D. Gelwicks.
Jameson's Ranch—
Wm. Jameson,
H. Fitzgerald.

FLOOR MANAGERS:
T. D. Heiskell,
E. Bogardus.

## SOCIAL BALL.

*Miss S. Hays*

The Pleasure of your Company is respectfully solicited at a Social Ball, to be given at the

### WILLOW SPRINGS HOUSE,

On Wednesday Evening, November 9th, 1853.

### MANAGERS:

WM. GOODE,
B. F WAYNE,
Dry Town.
M. MILLER,
Amadore.
Col. A. PLATT,
Sutter Creek.
A. A. HUMPHREYS,
Jackson.
J. P. DOUGLASS,
Mokelumne Hill.
MR. HANFORD,
Volcano.
JAS. BURT,
Fiddle Town.
T. D. HEISKILL,
Indian Diggings.
DR. O. P. WHITE,
Cedarville.
N. MOWREY,
Michigan Bar.
JOHN KNIGHT,
Big Bar.

J. R. MOBONE.
A. M. PLUMMER,
Cosumnes.
A. GILLMORE,
Forks Cosumnes.
WM. Z. WALKER,
O. PLUMMER,
Dry Creek
CHAS. STONE,
Buena Vista Ranch.
J. H. ALVORD,
J. MOORE,
Ione Valley.
WARNER,
Mountain House.
S. LINDSEY,
Somersett House.
C. S. COOVER,
H. A. CHASE,
A. PERRY,
R. MOREHOUSE,
Sac. City.

FLOOR MANAGERS:
DR. C. W. FOX.        F. WALKER.

## ANNIVERSARY BALL.

The pleasure of your Company is respectfully solicited at an Anniversary Ball, to be given at the

### WILLOW SPRINGS HOUSE,

On Thursday Evening Nov. 9th, 1854.

### MANAGERS:

Dr. C. W. Fox, Drytown;
G. W. Crandall, Sutter Creek;
A. A. Humphreys, Jackson;
C. Slort, Fiddletown;
F. B. Bicknell, Indian Diggings;
B. F. Wayne, Michigan Bar;
W. Davenport, Cook's Bar;
A. F. Bowman, Forks Cosumnes;
W. Driver, Cedarville;

A. M. Plumber, Cosumnes;
Chas. Stone, Buena Vista Ranch;
J. Martin, Ione Valley;
T. Luther,        "
J. Daks, Mountain House;
J. H. Alvord, Boston Store;
C. S. Coover, Sacramento;
H. A. Chace,        "
A. Perry,        "

FLOOR MANAGERS:
F. Walker.        O. Plumber.        J. R. Covel.

*Courtesy,* The Society of California Pioneers, San Francisco, Calif.

The view of Murphy's Diggings *above*, and the two views which follow it, were in their time the handsomest things of their kind made in California. Thirty subjects in all make up the full series produced between 1855 and 1858 by Charles Kuchel and Emil Dresel. Other prints from the series will be found toward the end of this chapter.

Note in this view of Angels Camp the number of quartz mills pictured in the border. When the placers were exhausted, Angels took a new lease on life as deep shafts tapped gold-bearing rock.

Downieville (*above* in 1856) was isolated on the North Yuba; necessary supplies were brought in from Marysville over seventy-odd miles of pack trails.

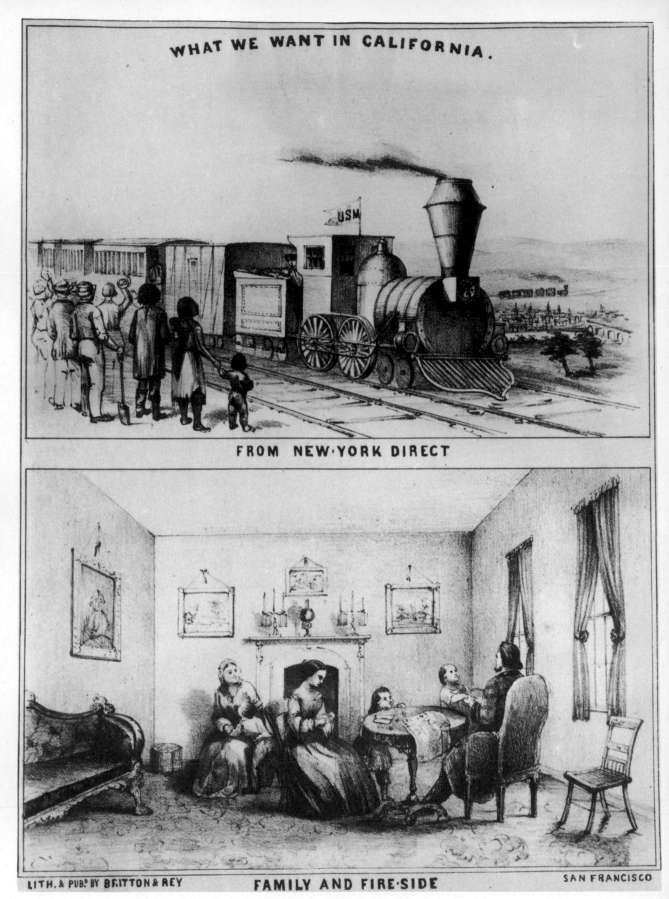

WHAT WE WANT IN CALIFORNIA.

FROM NEW·YORK DIRECT

FAMILY AND FIRE·SIDE

LITH. & PUB.ᴰ BY BRITTON & REY    SAN FRANCISCO

The utilitarian and the sentimental blended nicely in this broadside declaration of California's needs.

# METROPOLIS

For those who could skate without qualms on thin financial ice, the San Francisco of 1853 was a delightful place. A cheerful blindness to signs of imminent trouble characterized the outlook of most bankers, merchants and speculators.

This was still the San Francisco of George Horatio Derby's most boisterous practical jokes—a city liberal to musicians and actors—the city which was home to Barry and Patten's saloon, the Montgomery Street refuge where gathered a witty, generous and sophisticated crew. There the traveler might find Ferdinand Ewer from the Custom House, with the idea of the *Pioneer* buzzing in his brain— Kemble, junior editor of the *Alta*, very grand in his sombrero and fine raiment— "Jeems Pipes of Pipesville" (otherwise the versatile Stephen Massett)—Alonzo Delano—Frank Soule.

It was a city intellectual enough to give a new direction to American literature—witty enough to originate and savor that exquisite perversion of a line from *King Lear*, "How sharper than a serpent's thanks it is to have a toothless child"—juvenile enough to roar with appreciation at japes like Derby's description of the first meeting of the extremely respectable Ladies' Relief Society, a full-blooded fabrication in which "an elderly female in a Tuscan bonnet and green veil" buoyed herself up during the proceedings by, from time to time, "drawing a black pint bottle from the pocket of her dress" and taking "a snifter therefrom, with vast apparent satisfaction."

It was also a city of quick sentiment, from which a friend sent back east to the parents of a dead boy, the daguerreotype shown *below*—for whatever comfort the sight might give them.

*Courtesy,* The New-York Historical Society, New York City

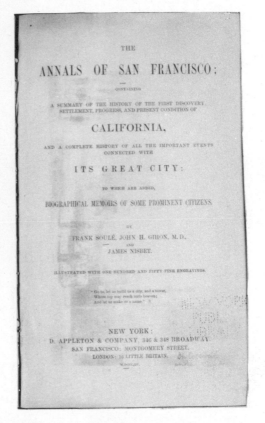

By the end of 1854, San Francisco had aged sufficiently to justify publication of its *Annals*, the story of men and events memorable in a short but crowded history. To the editors of this book, the purpose of history was to amass a delightful rubbish-heap of dislocated facts. Cheek by jowl are lurid tales of the primrose path, and sober reminders that the majority of the citizens were essentially virtuous. Praise was meted out to the benevolent activities of San Franciscans, and to the zeal with which material improvement went forward.

*Below* is the frontispiece to the *Annals*, an 1854 view of Montgomery Street, looking north from California Street. Brick and mortar had succeeded lath and canvas. "Blocks" of substantial buildings had been erected.

Both illustrations on this page are by the *courtesy* of The New York Public Library, New York City

SARONI, ARCHER & C?

UMBRELLAS, CANES, DRESSING CASES &

HATS, CAPS & GENTS FURNISHING STORE

*Courtesy,* The New-York Historical Society, New York City

The imposing shop front *above* stood on Clay Street between Montgomery and Kearny, prior to 1856. The original print was a lithograph in full color and was distributed to advertise the establishment.

*View on the Plaza (1856)*

*Courtesy,* The New-York Historical Society, New York City

In the view *above* of Portsmouth Square, or Plaza as one prefers, the Bella Union's facade stands out like a sore thumb. A little further to the right, the El Dorado may be seen, snuggling up against a corner of the City Hall.

The hour was about to strike for these establishments, and for carefree occupants of the City Hall whose favor supported them and haunts of worse repute. Through the lush years, except for the popular explosion of 1851, the people of San Francisco had accepted a low state of public morals as part of the price for greatness and speed of expansion. But as the depression of business grew worse through 1855, people became less tolerant of apathetic prosecutors, graft-swollen politicians, corrupted courts and shyster attorneys.

February, 1855, was the great month of financial collapse. Individual fortunes had already been swallowed up; now it was the turn of Page, Bacon and Company, Adams and Company, and other financial giants to suspend payment. Wild news of new gold strikes did not halt the progress of failure. The public mind began to think of reform; the public eye looked angrily about for scapegoats.

Kearney Street (1856)

James King "of William," so called to distinguish him from others similarly named, began a campaign of public enlightenment in the fall of 1855. His San Francisco *Bulletin* assailed by name the public officials whose connivance was to blame for the bawdy houses and the gambling houses and for a moral atmosphere in which swindling and embezzlement were condoned.

Could the bosses choose no better candidate for supervisor than a cheap, machine journalist and politician, who was a veteran of the New York State Penitentiary, asked King? The candidate replied to the question—with a gun. James Casey met King at the door of his office on the afternoon of May 14, 1856, fired a single shot into his victim's chest, watched him stagger into the office of the Pacific Express Company, and then permitted himself to be taken to jail.

King did not die until May 20. Meanwhile a new Vigilance Committee had been formed and its disciplined, armed companies supported the seizure of Casey and another murderer, one Charles Cora, from the unwilling hands of the legal Sheriff. On May 22, as King's funeral procession wound toward the cemetery, Casey and Cora were publicly hanged in front of the Vigilance Committee's meeting rooms on Sacramento Street.

Execution of *CASEY & CORA*,
by the San Francisco Vigilance Committee
May 22ª 1856.

*Courtesy*, The Huntington Library, San Marino, Calif.

The lithograph *above* tells its own story. Not all good citizens approved of the Committee's high-handed methods, and the Chief Justice of the State Supreme Court denounced the Committee's actions as a rebellion of "damned pork merchants." But as seen in the view *below* (based on one of the lost Vance daguerreotypes), mass meetings of San Franciscans turned out to endorse the suspension of normal legal process during the months of June and July.

*MASS MEETING*
Endorsing the Acts of the Vigilance Committe
June 14th

*Courtesy*, Edward Eberstadt & Sons, New York City

*"Fort Vigilance"*
*Head Quarters — Committee of Vigilance — 1856.*

The declared intention of the Second Vigilance Committee was to purge the city of ballot-box stuffers and criminals. To enforce law, it proposed to use illegal means—to hold suspects *incommunicado,* and in other ways to set itself up as the final authority. Its headquarters on Sacramento Street between Davis and Front was turned into a fortress (*above*) and received the nickname "Fort Gunnybags." Cannon were trained to command the approaches; the bell was ready to summon thousands of armed and devoted supporters.

But the tension gradually relaxed. After the execution of two more notorious murderers and the banishment of a few hard cases and corruptionists, the Committee wisely avoided conflict with Federal authority by voluntary retirement on August 18, 1856. Its best work was done after its demise—for thanks to its efforts, in the autumn elections a freely voting populace was able to sweep the old gang from office and by democratic action achieve necessary reforms in the city and the state.

FROM NATURE AND ON STONE BY KUCHEL & DRESEL, 176 CLAY St S.F.

STOC

PRINTED BY BRITTON & REY

TON.

Other towns, founded in the scurry and confusion of the search for gold, continued to thrive during the settling-down period. Compare this 1855 view of Stockton with the sketch on page 147.

SAN  J

The town of San Jose, where the first legislature of California had convened in 1849, was by 1858 the center of trade in the Santa Clara Valley. Note the signs—"Washington Hotel"—"City Drug Store."

From Nature & on Stone by Kuchel & Dresel

LOS AN

ꓶELES,

The waning of the obsession for gold and the diversification of California's economic life brought prosperity to some of the older towns. By the time this picture was made, Los Angeles was the center of a thriving trade in stock and had achieved some of the two-gun, brawling notoriety of the mining towns to the northward.

*Courtesy*, The Society of California Pioneers, San Francisco, Calif.

Far up on the northern end of Humboldt Bay, Union (*above*, on modern maps called Arcata) had become the depot for pack trains to the mines on the Klamath and the Trinity.

Kuchel and Dresel had their own methods for ensuring financial profit on their handsome pictures. Whether or not your home or place of business appeared on the border was determined by the number of prints for which you subscribed.

*Yerba Buena Island and the Bay between Sacramento, Jackson Streets*

Courtesy, The New-York Historical Society, New York City

The city of St. Francis lost no character or importance during that first decade in which California matured and stabilized. By 1854, the roving politicians of the state fixed on Sacramento for the capital, but San Francisco, on her lovely, westward-looking Bay, was not distressed. For she was fixed forever in the memories of the Argonauts; one way or another, she had been welcoming host to all who came. The tall clippers had dropped anchor in that harbor after the double of the Cape, the calms below the Line, the fogs. To her had come the steamers from the Isthmus, cram-packed with adventurers straining their eyes for a first sight of the land from which they expected so much. Down the rivers from the mines, launches and schooners had brought to her the veterans of the overland and the Gila, dust in their wallets, thirst in their throats, and filled with a consuming passion for the gayety and companionship of a city. Everyone had memories of San Francisco—she was as much a legend as the gold rush itself—a place long desired, a merry, heart-free place, a loud, bawdy place, a place which had become home to many and hell to some.

Her early glories and iniquities were now safely laid away in the lavender of the *Annals*—the fires, the mud, the rogues who had walked the streets, the fever of speculation. The Vigilance Committees had stacked arms and retired—their work was done, at any rate for the moment. Financial ruin had come, had been endured, and prosperity had returned—a milder, less exuberant prosperity, but much more real and less often seen as the adornment of flamboyant rascals. The city stood on the threshold of greatness, as premier port and financial center of the Pacific Coast for many years to come.

City and state were one in their zest for the fullness of life. None of the Forty-Niners found acres of candied roses on which to feast in idleness, but out of the perils of the transit, the work which calloused their hands and bent their backs, the indomitable will with which they strove against the pressures of disaster, their descendants and the nation derived a symbol of strength—the pioneer, of whom Walt Whitman said:

> *Come my tan-faced children,*
> *Follow well in order, get your weapons ready;*
> *Have you your pistols? have you your sharp-edged axes?*
> *Pioneers! O pioneers!*
>
> *For we cannot tarry here,*
> *We must march my darlings, we must bear the brunt of danger,*
> *We, the youthful sinewy races, all the rest on us depend,*
> *Pioneers! O pioneers!*
>
> *O you, youths, Western youths,*
> *So impatient, full of action, full of manly pride and friendship,*
> *Plain I see you, Western youths, see you tramping with the foremost,*
> *Pioneers! O pioneers!*
>
> *Have the elder races halted?*
> *Do they droop and end their lesson, wearied, over there beyond the seas?*
> *We take up the task eternal, and the burden, and the lesson,*
> *Pioneers! O pioneers!*
>
> *All the past we leave behind;*
> *We debouch upon a newer, mightier world, varied world,*
> *Fresh and strong the world we seize, world of labor and the march,*
> *Pioneers! O pioneers!*

# INDEX

# INDEX

1

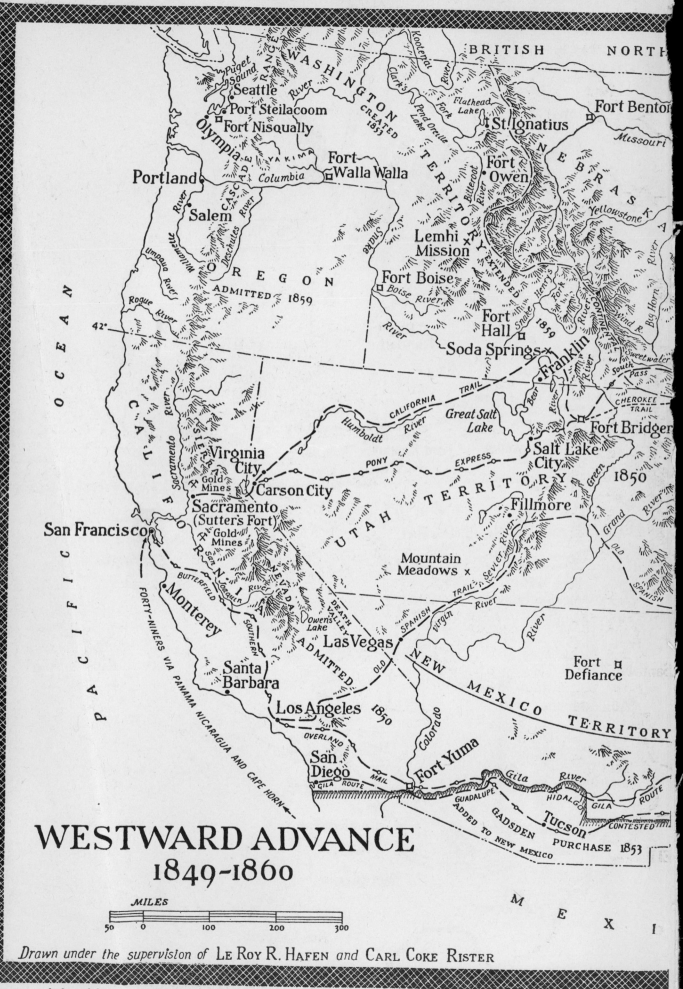

# WESTWARD ADVANCE
## 1849-1860

MILES

50  0  100  200  300

*Drawn under the supervision of* LE ROY R. HAFEN *and* CARL COKE RISTER